"Elizabeth Collier and Charles Strain's *Global Migration: What's Happening, Why, and a Just Response* brings together key resources to analyze the complex factors confronting people on the move today. The authors skillfully illuminate Christian witness from biblical texts through Catholic social teaching to lived responses. They also underscore the critical need to understand root causes and contexts of migration, not just its symptoms. The book's 'see-judge-act' framework guides readers to a range of innovative responses. This book serves as an excellent resource for classrooms, immersion trips, parish-based discussion groups, or nonprofit organizations."

—Kristin Heyer
Boston College

"*Global Migration: What's Happening, Why, and a Just Response*, by Elizabeth Collier and Charles Strain, is an invaluable resource for foundational information, human formation, and social transformation. The authors remind us that migration is not the central problem but rather the symptom of deeper imbalances that uproot people and cause them to move. The authors also challenge us to move beyond incendiary debates to the central moral issues, reminding us that the moral wealth of a country begins with how it treats its most vulnerable members. In bringing out the humanity of the immigrant, Collier and Strain call us to reflect on who we are before God, who we are in this journey of life, and who we are in response to our neighbor in need."

—Daniel G. Groody, CSC
University of Notre Dame

Author Acknowledgments

We gratefully acknowledge those who helped with the development and review of this project at Anselm Academic and Catholic Relief Services, in particular, Bradley Harmon, Maura Hagarty, Beth Erickson, Kim Lamberty, and Louis Charest, as well as Wen-der Lin, Brian Bartels, and the media production staff at DePaul University.

Publisher Acknowledgment

Thank you to the following individual who reviewed this work in progress:

Daniel G. Groody, CSC, *University of Notre Dame*

Global Migration

WHAT'S HAPPENING, WHY, AND A JUST RESPONSE

Elizabeth W. Collier and Charles R. Strain

with Catholic Relief Services

Dedication

To the staff at Catholic Relief Services, who tirelessly work with and on behalf of the most vulnerable people in the world, and to the educators who work to inspire students to create a more just and humane world.

Created by the publishing team of Anselm Academic.

The scriptural quotations contained herein are from the New Revised Standard Version of the Bible. Copyright © 1993 and 1989 by the Division of Christian Education of the National Council of the Churches of Christ in the United States of America. All rights reserved.

Cover images: © Kira Horvath for CRS

Printed in the United States of America

7080

ISBN 978-1-59982-894-7

Contents

Introduction

Stories That Shape Our Lives

In the Abrahamic religious traditions—Judaism, Christianity, and Islam—faith is often described as the courage to move and, in moving, become someone new. The motif of migration appears throughout these traditions' sacred texts. Abram is called by God to leave the city of Ur and migrate to a new home where he will become Abraham, our common father (Gen. 12:1–9). In the book of Exodus, the Israelites follow Moses out of Egypt and slavery and into the wilderness. They are not without fear and complaints, but they persist until they reach the Promised Land. As the account continues, Yahweh commands the Israelites, "When an alien resides with you in your land, you shall not oppress the alien. The alien who resides with you shall be to you as the citizen among you; you shall love the alien as yourself, for you were aliens in the land of Egypt" (Lev. 19:33–34).

In the Gospel of Matthew, Joseph hearkens to the warning of an angel and flees into Egypt with Mary and Jesus to escape Herod's sword. Like so many today who are forced to leave everything behind to escape persecution, the Holy Family seeks asylum. Paul, in the Letter to the Hebrews, raises hospitality toward the stranger to a sacred act, saying, "By doing that some have entertained angels without knowing it" (Heb. 13:2).

Hijrah, the migration of the Prophet Mohammed, is central to the Islamic faith. In May 622 CE, the Prophet Mohammed fled from Mecca to Yathrib (later renamed Medina), escaping an assassination plot. The welcome and protection that the people of Yathrib offered to the Prophet became a model for Muslims' hospitality to the stranger.

Ancestors of many living in the United States today were forced to emigrate against their will: African slaves were chained together in the holds of sailing ships. Others fled to America to escape impossible living conditions in their country of origin: one million Irish men and women left their homeland during the famine of the mid-1840s, and many Jews fled pogroms in Russia. Fleeing poverty or persecution, more than twenty-seven million people migrated to the United States between 1880 and 1930.[1] All people living in the United States, including Native Americans, have a migration story—maybe recent, maybe many generations past. "When we forget our personal and collective migration stories," Daniel Groody argues, "immigrants easily become the targets of social problems and are quickly typecast as a threat to the common good." When people break bread together in the Eucharist, he adds, they remember both the centrality of migration in scriptural tradition and their own stories of migration.[2]

Migration continues to be a global phenomenon. At the latest count, 244 million people reside in a nation in which they were not born. While some are concerned about the level of migration to the United States, the reality is that while the United States is host to the largest number of foreign-born people (46.6 million), numerous other countries have welcomed a greater percentage of immigrants relative to their overall population (e.g., Canada's 22 percent to the United States' 15.2 percent).[3]

Another 65.3 million people currently live in forced displacement because of war, political repression, or religious persecution either as *refugees* or *asylum seekers* in a new country or as *internally displaced persons* within their native land. In 2016, one half of all refugees came from three nations: Syria, Afghanistan, and Somalia. The Syrian refugee crisis is only the latest source of massive forced migration. The European Union and the United States have not borne a proportionate burden of this vast stream of migrants. Turkey has sheltered 2.5 million Syrian refugees; Lebanon, 1.1 million; and Jordan, 664,000. These countries have limited resources to address the needs of their own populations, let alone the masses in need of a place of refuge. Overall, 86 percent of refugees reside in developing nations.[4]

---

1. "Immigration Timeline," The Statue of Liberty—Ellis Island Foundation, Inc., *www.libertyellisfoundation.org/immigration-timeline*.

2. Daniel Groody, "Fruit of the Vine and Work of Human Hands," in *A Promised Land: A Perilous Journey*, ed. Daniel Groody and Gioacchino Campese (Notre Dame, IN: University of Notre Dame Press, 2008): 302–3.

3. United Nations High Commissioner for Refugees, "Global Trends 2015: Forced Displacement Hits a Record High," *www.unhcr.org/en-us/global-trends-2015*; International Organization for Migration, "Global Migration Trends 2015 Fact Sheet," *http://publications.iom.int/books/global-migration-trends-factsheet-2015*.

4. Ibid.

Key Terms

Refugee A person who, "owing to well-founded fear of being persecuted for reasons of race, religion, nationality, membership of a particular social group or political opinion, is outside the country of his [sic] nationality and is unable or, owing to such fear, is unwilling to avail himself of the protection of that country."[5]

Asylum seeker A person who has left his or her country of origin, in accordance with the definition of "refugee" and formally presented him or herself at or within the border of another country for asylum.

Internally displaced person A person who has been forced to leave his or her home because of armed conflict, situations of generalized violence, or violations of human rights, but who has not crossed an internationally recognized state border.

Economic migrant A person who has moved to another country to find employment in the absence of opportunities in his or her homeland.

These figures do not include the average 22.5 million human beings who have migrated in each of the past eight years because of extreme weather events or natural disasters. Given climate change and an increase in extreme weather events, this figure will undoubtedly grow.[6]

If these immigrants, refugees, asylum seekers, internally displaced people and migrants fleeing natural disasters were gathered in one place, they would form the third largest nation on Earth (331.8 million), surpassing the entire population of the United States (322.8 million). While many people find a place in another country to begin a new life, there are still millions in desperate circumstances. Their suffering requires a better response from the worldwide community.

---

5. United Nations High Commissioner for Refugees, "Convention and Protocol Relating to the Status of Refugees," 1951, *www.unhcr.org/en-us/3b66c2aa10*.

6. United Nations High Commissioner for Refugees, "Human Mobility in the Context of Climate Change UNFCCC-Paris COP-21," *www.unhcr.org/en-us /565b21bd9.pdf*.

Method: See, Judge, Act

This book employs the "see-judge-act" method for exploring global migration in its multiple shapes and forms. This method was first developed by French priests working with young workers seeking justice during the 1950s in a movement called Catholic Action. The method was further developed in Latin America in the late 1960s, as priests, nuns, and lay catechists convened small groups of peasants to grapple with unjust structures oppressing the vulnerable. It continues to be widely used to structure ethical reflection on social issues for the purpose of working for justice.

See

The first step in the see-judge-act method is to "see" what is going on in a situation. Pope Francis calls us to see with the eyes of faith. "Globalization is a phenomenon that challenges us," he argues, "especially in one of its principal manifestations, which is emigration. It is one of the 'signs' of this time that we live in and that brings us back to the words of Jesus, 'Why do you not know how to interpret the present time?'"[7] The stories of how Jesus approached or received people in the Gospels provide an example of how he "saw" people. He saw and perceived in greater depth in people than what initially met the eyes of those in the biblical scene.

When looking upon good friends or close family members, most people see what those individuals are going through as part of the larger whole of their lives. This includes their aspirations, gifts and talents, potential, and the circumstances that have led them to a particular moment. The task in the "seeing" step in this text is to view the world through the eyes of migrants and their communities—examining both what one knows and does not know about the experience of migrants. "Seeing" requires asking many questions in order to understand why people uproot themselves and their families.[8]

7. "Pope Calls for Protection of Unaccompanied Child Migrants," Vatican Radio, July 16, 2014, *http://en.radiovaticana.va/news/2014/07/15/pope_calls_for_protection_of_unaccompanied_child_migrants_/1102879*.

8. Deacon Steve Swope, "Understanding Syrian Refuges, One Story at a Time," Catholic Relief Services, February 11, 2016, *www.crs.org/media-center/understanding-syrian-refugees-one-story-time*.

Human beings generally do not leave family, culture, language, and "home" to start anew in a wholly different culture, unless they are under extreme duress.[9]

With social media and 24/7 cable news, people are flooded with information, faceless numbers, and images of refugees on rickety boats in rough seas or migrants crossing the Arizona desert to reunite with family or find jobs. But much of what is reported does not help people truly "see" what is happening. A Vietnamese Buddhist monk, Thich Nhat Hanh, exiled in France because of political persecution, suggests that, despite all of the information available, "America is somehow a closed society."[10] Americans live in what some social scientists call "lifestyle enclaves," where people associate primarily with others of the same class, level of education, or race. Many do not have direct contact with refugees or migrants. Even with millions of people on the move around the world, most others do not really know the migrants' stories.

Understanding the realities of migration is difficult. Every migration story is the result of a complex set of social, economic, political, and geographic forces, which we may barely comprehend. Often a tragic story lies behind the migrants' decision to leave their place of origin. Though every migrant's story is unique, when we "see" the situations of particular individuals we discover features of many migrants' stories. Truly seeing what is behind the migration of peoples requires educating oneself, imagining oneself in similar situations,[11] and asking questions about particular migrants. Appropriate questions include the following:

- Why have these people uprooted themselves from the culture, language, and homeland of their family?
- What are the political, economic, environmental, and social forces that made living in their homeland untenable or dehumanizing?

9. "First-ever Refugee Team Joins Summer Olympics," Catholic Relief Services, *www.crs.org/stories/first-ever-refugee-team-joins-summer-olympics.*

10. Thich Nhat Hanh, *Being Peace* (Berkeley, CA: Parallax, 1995), 181.

11. Kevin Hartigan, "5 Questions and Answers on 5-Year Anniversary of Syrian Civil War," Catholic Relief Services, *www.crs.org/media-center/5-year-anniversary -syrian-civil-war-5-questions-answers.*

- What, if any, living alternatives do these people have within their own country's borders?
- What stories do these people tell about their plight at home? About their migration? About their lives after relocating?

Through community-based learning courses, teachers provide students with opportunities to "see" some of the realities associated with migration and to answer some of these questions within the context of a course. Some students have served in organizations that help refugees resettle in the United States. They greet people at the airport when they arrive from a refugee camp, get them settled into an apartment, teach them the basics of apartment living in the United States, and then try to support them during the ninety days that the government allots for them to learn English and get jobs. Students have worked for organizations that advocate for immigration reform in the United States. Others have taken study trips to the United States-Mexico border, where they met with migrants and studied the forces behind migration from Mexico or Central America to the United States.

This book ties its analyses of global migration to actual people, many of them supported by the work of Catholic Relief Services (CRS). CRS is the international relief and development agency of the Catholic community in the United States. CRS carries out the commitment of the Catholic bishops in the United States to assist the poor and vulnerable overseas. It has projects in more than one hundred countries serving more than 107 million people in 2015.[12] This book offers numerous examples of the work CRS has done in the field.[13]

---

12. CRS, "Where Two or Three Are Gathered in My Name . . . Annual Report 2015," *http://annualreport.crs.org/wp-content/uploads/2016/06/CRS_AR_2015.pdf.*

13. CRS offers options for students to break out of their enclaves by working with or creating campus organizations that deal with issues of global migration, such as the CRS Student Ambassador Program. On the work of CRS, see "Mission Statement," *www.crs .org/about/mission-statement,* and "Our Work Overseas," *www.crs.org/our-work-overseas;* on CRS student ambassadors, see "About Student Ambassadors," *university.crs.org /students/about.*

Young Refugees and Migrants

Fifty-one percent of refugees are children under the age of eighteen. Only half of these children have access to primary education in their current living situations and only one in four adolescents has access to secondary education.[14]

Sakeena Mteir is eleven years old. She loves to draw. She is also a refugee, one of 4.8 million Syrians who have fled violence in their homeland. For four years, she, her parents, and eight siblings have lived in a makeshift shelter in Lebanon. Not only has CRS supported more than one million Syrian refugees, but it has also sponsored a summer camp where children, including Sakeena, make puppets and put on puppet shows. The shows enable children to express the trauma of being uprooted from their homes and schools. "The puppets are very important for the children because children relate to puppets as if they were human beings," a CRS fieldworker says. "We discovered that this method is very good because it helps them talk about feelings, which they usually can't talk about easily."[15]

Sakeena Mteir

© Nikki Gamer / CRS

continued

14. United Nations High Commissioner for Refugees, "UNHCR 2015 Global Child Protection, Education and SGBV Strategy Implementation Report," *www.unhcr .org/en-us/publications/fundraising/57612a017/2015-global-child-protection-education -sgbv-strategy-implementation-report.html*; United Nations High Commissioner for Refugees, "No Lost Generation 2015 Syrian Refugee Crisis Update: Moving to a New Phase in the NLG," *https://data.unhcr.org/syrianrefugees/download.php?id=10210*.

15. Nikki Gamer, "A CRS Summer Camp for Syrian Refugees Helps Kids Be Kids," Catholic Relief Services, *http://crs.org/stories/crs-summer-camp-syrian-refugees -helps-kids-be-kids*; Barb Fraze, "When Puppets Meet Refugees, Healing Begins for Children," Catholic News Service, *www.catholicnews.com/services/englishnews/2014 /when-puppets-meet-refugees-healing-begins-for-children.cfm*.

> **Young Refugees and Migrants** *continued*
>
> Fermin Mendoza is an undocumented migrant. He is one of more than a million migrants brought to America as a child by his parents. He reflects upon his experience in ninth grade:
>
> > First day of geography class. Ninth grade. I know little about geography, but I am excited to learn. . . . I pick a front-row seat and study the large world map on the wall. . . . Mr. Giordana . . . gives our first assignment. One at a time, everyone will reveal their birthplaces. I stare off into the whiteboard, scared. No one in the room knows that I was born in Mexico. People start giving simple answers I wish I could use. Houston. San Antonio. . . . I think about the name of my birthplace: Gustavo Diaz Ordaz, Tamaulipas . . . Mexico. . . . I don't even know where my hometown is. It's my turn to share now. *Diaz Ordas, Tamaulipas,* I tell Mr. Giordano. *Is that a big city?* he asks. *Yes,* I lie. *I've never heard of it,* he replies. The next student speaks. I wonder if the class knows I am illegal.[16]

Judge

The second step in the see-judge-act process is evaluative. It involves taking the stories, data, research, and knowledge gained in step one and analyzing them through the most appropriate lenses, as well as through the theological and ethical lenses that Catholic social teaching (CST) provides. The chapters of part 1 provide some analysis, particularly when working through several arguments for and against migration to the United States. The sole chapter in part 2 discusses the main tenets of CST, their relationship to migration, and the five rights of migrants that CST puts forth. CST maintains that people should consult additional sources of wisdom in order to achieve a well-rounded understanding of the issues. These additional sources,

---

16. Ingrid Hernandez, Fermin Mendoza, Mario Lio, Jirayut Latthi, and Catherine Eusibio, "Things I'll Never Say: Stories of Growing Up Undocumented in the United States," *Harvard Educational Review* 81, no. 3 (Fall 2011): 502.

drawn from economics, psychology, criminal justice, and sociology, help in the application of the CST tenets. Part 2 also explores some moral challenges and encourages the reader to sort through them and make judgments. Questions that are important to ask in this step include the following:

- How can claims made by people involved in global migration be researched in order to validate or discredit the arguments?
- Whose voices dominate in discussions about global migration? Why?
- Whose voices are missing? Why?
- What do migrants, refugees, and those who work closely with them recommend in order to improve the situation of migrants?
- In what ways does global migration enhance or diminish human dignity?
- What issues of justice are raised by the global economic order's impact on migration? What is the relationship between the global economy and patterns of migration? What issues of justice does this relationship raise?
- What is the responsibility of Christian communities for addressing the plight of refugees?
- What is your own evaluation of the core principles of CST? How do they fit with your own moral framework?

By answering these questions and others sparked by deep listening in the "see" step, we move through the judgment step in such a way that we can propose actions that individuals, organizations, and communities of people can take to address injustice or dehumanizing situations.

What judgments does this cartoon convey? What images does it use to convey them? What analogies does it draw? How does the cartoonist view migration?

Act

After completing the "see" and "judge" steps and carefully considering what has been learned, the next step is to determine how to act in response. Actions can be either individual or collective.

Collective Action

Collective actions can be carried out by small communities, nongovernmental organizations (NGOs), and nations. For example, American citizens may ask what the United States is morally obligated to do in the face of a refugee crisis like that created by the Syrian civil war or, closer to home, the crisis of refugees fleeing violence in Central America or of people being displaced by climate change. This book focuses on strategies and projects developed through collective action by CRS and its overseas partners.

Individual Action

The fact that the global refugee crisis and the current stalemate regarding comprehensive immigration reform in the United States both require collective action by governments and nongovernmental organizations does not relieve individuals of their responsibility to act as moral agents. In the "act" step, individuals consider the following questions in light of the findings of the seeing and judging steps:

- Which needed actions am I capable of doing? Which actions match up with my gifts, talents, or resources?
- What is a realistic level of commitment for me?
- With whom will I work? Will I work alone or with my family or faith community, or as part of a local organization or larger nonprofit?
- If no formal structure exists within which I can work, with whom can I network in order to set something up?

An Invitation

Action without ethical reflection is blind, but ethical reflection without action is sterile. This text invites readers to become aware of the complexities of global migration ("see"), to make judgments based upon ethical concepts and principles ("judge"), and to respond in some way, however small ("act").

Reflect and Discuss

1. Do any stories from religious traditions help you make sense of human migration? If you have a faith tradition, what does it say about how to greet and treat the stranger?

2. Interview someone who is a recent immigrant, perhaps a member of your family or a friend. What is their story? What led them to migrate and what kind of welcome did they receive when they came here? What is your own family's migration story?

3. View the linked video on forced displacement: "Global Trends 2015 Video," United Nations High Commissioner for Refugees, *www.unhcr.org/en-us/news/videos/2016/6/5763b73c4/global-trends-2015-video* (time: 0:05:00). How does hearing the stories and viewing the faces behind the statistics help you develop your own ethical evaluation of this human tragedy?

PART 1

See—Understanding Global Migration

The most pressing ethical issues today involve a complex web of economic, social, historical, religious, and political realities that can be difficult to grasp. While many people have opinions about issues like immigration, few fully understand the factors that lead people to uproot themselves and their families, and the difficulties of relocating and settling in humanizing environments. Part 1 gives a general overview of the factors that result in migration, the barriers migrants face in resettling, and the inaccuracies in many arguments put forth in the public sphere by those who are not educated on such matters.

CHAPTER 1

Meeting the Challenges of the World's Refugees

Miriam is a sixteen-year-old Catholic girl from Iraq. She and her family fled Iraq when ISIS invaded their region in 2014. She is one of 65.3 million people forcibly displaced from their homes who are currently living as refugees, asylum seekers, or internally displaced peoples (IDP). This is a staggering figure—roughly the population of California and Texas. To say that the resources of the United Nations High Commissioner for Refugees (UNHCR) and the hundreds of nongovernmental organizations (NGOs) that work with the UNHCR are stretched to the breaking point is a grave understatement.

Miriam missed a year of school while her family reestablished itself in Jordan. Like other children, she has aspirations. She wants

This Syrian family waits for a bus that will take them to Hungary. The family, seeking asylum in Germany, has been traveling for more than a month.

to become a pediatrician. "If you don't study and get a degree," she says, "you can't have a life." Thanks to Caritas Jordan, a partner of Catholic Relief Services (CRS), Miriam is one of a lucky few who are back in school.[1]

Miriam's story brings home another point: food, clothing, and shelter are not enough. Children—and one half of all refugees or IDPs are children—cannot lose four years or more of education without harming their development, their families, and their communities. How is this developmental need to be met?

Evolution of International Law and the Rights of Refugees[2]

The story of the world community's attempts to respond to the needs of refugees like Miriam begins with the end of World War II. The horrors of the Nazi Holocaust, visited upon Jews and other minorities, led to several developments in international law, as well as the creation of organizations like CRS that help migrants and refugees. The most notable development was creation of the Universal Declaration of Human Rights. The ongoing sufferings of refugees from World War II who had not yet been integrated into a new country prompted the United Nations (UN) to create a Convention on the Status of Refugees and charged the UNHCR with carrying it out. Ratified in 1951, the Convention declares, as the most basic right of refugees, the right not to be returned to the country where they face threats to their lives and liberty, also known as non-refoulement.[3]

---

1. See "Miriam's Story: Finding Hope in Education," Catholic Relief Services, *www.crs.org/resource-center/miriams-story-finding-hope-education* (time: 0:04:27).

2. For the historical background on international law related to refugees and the evolution of the UNHCR's mandate, see Susan F. Martin, "Rethinking the International Refugee Regime in Light of Human Rights and the Global" in *Driven from Home: Protecting the Rights of Forced Migrants*, ed. David Hollenbach, SJ (Washington, DC: Georgetown University Press, 2010), 21–28; Astri Suhrke and Kathleen Newland, "UNHCR: Uphill into the Future," *The International Migration Review* 35, no. 1 (September 2001): 284–302.

3. For the legal definition of a refugee, see the United Nations High Commissioner for Refugees, "Convention and Protocol Relating to the Status of Refugees," 1951, article 1, *www.unhcr.org/en-us/3b66c2aa10*. A protocol adopted in 1967 removed time constraints attached to the original convention. See the introduction of this book for the Convention's definition of a refugee.

The Convention did not obligate states to admit refugees as legal permanent residents or to grant refugees citizenship. The Convention did, however, obligate states to guarantee several additional rights:

- The right not to be punished for illegal entry (article 31)
- The right to freedom of movement (article 26)
- The right to work (articles 17–19)
- The right to education (article 22)

The host countries do not always honor these rights. For example, it is common for refugees to be restricted to camps. In the United States, asylum seekers are routinely detained for months in local jails and prisons, in clear violation of the rights established by the Convention, before their cases are resolved.[4]

The 1951 Convention had a limited focus on European refugees of World War II. The United Nations High Commissioner for Refugees broadened its mission when it responded to calls for helping refugees who fled after Soviet troops crushed uprisings in Hungary (1956) and Czechoslovakia (1968). Two regional conventions covering Africa and the Americas broadened the definition of refugees to include those fleeing from foreign aggression, civil war, or "generalized violence." In the case of large-scale, forced migration, it was difficult to distinguish between those fleeing from political persecution and those simply escaping violence; in practice, the UNHCR treated all as refugees. During the Cold War, the Western nations saw a propaganda advantage in liberally granting asylum to refugees from the Soviet bloc. After the collapse of the Soviet Union, Western countries became less interested in granting asylum. Refugees are now much more likely to remain for long periods of time without their status resolved because there is no one willing to accept them permanently.

Since the end of the Cold War, the nature of war has changed. Wars are more likely to involve internal conflicts between different ethnic groups, as in the war in the former Yugoslavia in the 1990s. These wars primarily target civilians. This has led to massive

---

4. Sioban Albiol, "Immigrants and Refugees Held in Detention," in *Religious and Ethical Perspectives on Global Migration*, ed. Elizabeth Collier and Charles R. Strain (Lanham, MD: Lexington, 2014): 307–26.

migrations, but more often within countries than across international borders. The only difference, then, between most IDPs and refugees is whether or not they have crossed a border. Increasingly, the UNHCR has worked with IDPs. So far, UN member states have not expanded the mandate of the UNHCR to aid those forced to move because of natural disasters or climate change.

New Trends in Forced Migration

Besides the unprecedented numbers of migrants forced to flee and the growing proportion of children among them, several other trends have become evident:

- Protracted refugee situations are now the norm; their average duration is twenty-five years. Entire generations are born and raised to adulthood in some camps. Few of these refugees are able to return home or gain permanent asylum in a new country.
- A majority of refugees (60 percent) now live in cities. They see camps as dead ends.[5]
- An overwhelming percentage of refugees (86 percent) reside in developing countries. For example, most Syrian refugees live in Jordan, Lebanon, or Turkey. These countries have limited resources to assist such large numbers of people.
- In these protracted circumstances, only a few people will receive work permits, despite this being a right guaranteed to refugees by the Convention. Consequently, those in cities work in the underground economy and are frequently exploited.[6]
- Many advocates for the rights of migrants are contesting the dichotomy between forced and voluntary migration, implied by the Convention, which restricts the former to those fleeing war or political persecution. Advocates are asking how bad economic conditions or the impact of climate change need to be for migrants before they can be considered factors in "forced" migration.

---

5. Elizabeth Whitman, "We Can't Live in a Camp," *The Nation* (May 13, 2013): 244–26.

6. Catholic Relief Services, "Meeting the Challenges of the World's Refugee Crisis: Policy Brief," 1, 3–4, *www.crs.org/get-involved/advocate/public-policy/meeting -challenges-worlds-refugee-crisis-policy-brief*; Maryanne Loughry, "The Experience of Displacement by Conflict," in *Driven from Home*, ed. Hollenbach, 170–75.

In light of these trends, CRS, along with many other governmental and nongovernmental organizations, has been calling for an overhaul in how the world community addresses refugee crises. CRS offers the following guidelines to address the evolving needs of refugees:

- States should work through the UN to create new conventions that deal with types of forced migration that do not fit the current categories of international law.
- Humanitarian relief should be linked with development aid. Donors should shift from short-term, emergency aid to coupling such aid with longer-term projects (3–5 years) that enable refugees to become self-sufficient and contribute to their host communities.
- The UNHCR and NGOs that provide humanitarian aid should, where possible, work through local organizations. They should assess and build capacity for local, market-based solutions.
- Governments of wealthy nations must ease the burden placed on developing nations hosting refugees, and all aid groups should work to create positive linkages between host countries and refugee communities, including "non-camp solutions."[7]

Above all, these guidelines reflect a critical shift from viewing and treating refugees as victims to viewing and treating them as *agents*. For our focus on the ethics of migration, this shift—now widely accepted by NGOs providing aid to refugees—is the most crucial point. Media bombard viewers with images of refugees appearing as victims in dire circumstances—crowded on small boats, wading to shore, standing in packed lines for food, and these images often move people to offer help. Depicting refugees only as victims, however, risks stripping them of their dignity as agents who are committed to shaping their lives every bit as much as others. In fact, refugees take decisive action in leaving home, at great personal cost, to find safety elsewhere. Forms of charity that view refugees as merely recipients of others' generosity rather than as persons with the potential to contribute to the common good are inadequate from a

---

7. Catholic Relief Services, "Meeting the Challenges of the World's Refugee Crisis," 2, 9–12.

Christian perspective, as they fail to respect the God-given dignity of all people.

M. Brinton Lykes offers the case of Guatemalan women who were internally displaced or became refugees in Mexican camps during the thirty-six-year civil war (1960–1996) in that country as an example of self-empowering agency. These indigenous women formed groups to learn how to read and write; they discussed women's rights and health issues; they organized themselves and provided input on the return process after the war's end. While they faced a patriarchal backlash when they returned home, many persisted in educating themselves and staying politically active. Lykes concludes that to enable refugees to actualize the power that they have as agents involves "a focus on three areas: human capacity (i.e., skills, knowledge, and capabilities), social ecology (i.e., social connectedness and networks), and culture and values."[8]

An Unchecked Humanitarian Crisis

Huge flows of refugees from Syria, with additional refugees from the wars in Afghanistan and Iraq, precipitated a humanitarian crisis in 2015 and 2016 that revealed the weaknesses of the current refugee relief system. As the civil war in Syria grew worse, refugees became increasingly desperate. The pressure of refugees seeking asylum in European Union countries created global awareness of the crisis, but also a backlash by reactionary movements. The ambivalence of the West meant a lack of adequate response to the situation of the masses of refugees in the countries of Jordan, Lebanon, and Turkey. When then prime minister of the United Kingdom David Cameron announced that England would offer asylum to 20,000 Syrians—twice the number pledged by the United States—he was told that Lebanon had provided protection to that many in only the past two weekends.[9] In Jordan and Lebanon there are signs of local populations suffering under the strain

---

8. M. Brinton Lykes, "No Easy Road to Freedom: Engendering and Enculturating Forced Migration," in *Driven from Home*, ed. Hollenbach, 78–80.

9. David Hollenbach, SJ, "The Rights of Refugees," *America* (January 4, 2016): 14–17.

of the influx, such as rising rents forcing out local populations, unskilled local labor losing jobs to refugees, and a rise in consumer prices.[10] The affluent countries of the West have yet to significantly ease the burden imposed on these countries that neighbor Iraq and Syria.

Refugees are witnesses to humanity's common complicity in the world's suffering. Some of the forces that displace peoples are not separate from the economic and political structures that have created today's global society. "What displaced populations reveal to us all," argues Clement Mijawa, "are the profound shifts and stresses underlying our socioeconomic systems. . . . Refugee movements are like earthquakes. . . . They are the warning signs of the deep tensions within our global community."[11] It is incumbent upon each person and upon communities to acknowledge their complicity in the economic and climate forces that result in migration. These are issues of "commission." What are people *doing* in their daily lives that contributes to or exacerbates those issues that result in people needing to migrate? What trade policies, consumption trends, and business practices contribute to the problems that require people to move?

While much of the rhetoric in the Christian tradition on sin tends to focus on what people have done, the complicity involved in *failing to help* is as serious as committing a sinful act. While the New Testament story of the Good Samaritan (Luke 10:25–37) is often interpreted as a parable about the Samaritan helping the beaten traveler, the story also draws attention to those who *failed* to help. Refugees and migrants are in situations where they are very much dependent upon the responses of others. The Good Samaritan story challenges everyone to ask, "How have I responded? How can I respond?"

---

10. Cathrine Thorleifsson, "The Limits of Hospitality: Coping Strategies among Displaced Syrians in Lebanon," *Third World Quarterly* 37, no. 6 (February 2016): 1071–82; Roger Zetter and Heloise Ruaudel, "Development and Protection Challenges of the Syrian Refugee Crisis," *Revista Migraciones Forzadas* 47 (September, 2014): 6–10.

11. As cited in Agbonkhianmeghe E. Orobator, "Justice for the Displaced: The Challenge of a Christian Understanding," in *Driven from Home*, ed. Hollenbach, 42–43, 45. See also M. Brinton Lykes, "No Easy Road to Freedom: Engendering and Enculturating Forced Migration," in *Driven from Home*, ed. Hollenbach, 81.

Despite the challenges associated with migration, there are bright spots. Miriam is in school in Jordan pursuing her dream. In Egypt, a CRS project that provides business and legal training, allocates start-up capital, and increases technical skills is helping one Syrian woman to open a perfume shop, and another a beauty salon, and a Syrian man to reestablish his engine repair shop. "The goal is to go beyond short-term help and give refugees the tools and resources they need to become productive, self-reliant members of Egyptian society," says Yumiko Texidor, the CRS project director.[12] Given the immensity of the task, these changes may seem pitifully small. But they transform whole worlds, one person at a time.

Reflect and Discuss

1. What do Miriam's story and the stories of refugees in Egypt tell us about how refugees should be treated?

2. View the CRS video "Emergency Response and Recovery," *www.crs.org/our-work-overseas/program-areas/shelter-and -settlements* (time: 0:06:41), and then do the following:

   a. Explain the five principles that guide CRS's response to the immediate needs of those driven from their homes.

   b. Assess these principles in light of the CRS guidelines for responding to the migrants' needs as presented in this chapter.

   c. Identify the values reflected in the five principles.

3. What has changed in the global situation regarding forced migration between March 2017 (the publication date of this book) and the time you read this chapter? Is war still the major driver or are other forces like climate change creating greater pressures to migrate? What moral obligations do people face in light of new developments in forced migration? Do the principles advocated by CRS still apply?

---

12. Nikki Gamer, "Syrian Refugees: Starting Up and Starting Over," Catholic Relief Services, May 2, 2016, *www.crs.org/stories/syrian-refugees-starting-up-starting-over*.

CHAPTER 2

Climate Change "Refugees"

The Isle de Jean Charles is disappearing. Rising sea levels, resulting from climate change's impact on glaciers, have consumed 98 percent of the island's mass.[1] This is not a distant, exotic, Pacific island. It is part of the state of Louisiana. The sixty people whose ancestors have lived on the island since the 1830s are now relocating inland. Headlines have called them "America's first climate refugees." These people are members of the Choctaw nation, one of five Native American nations that Presidents Andrew Jackson and Martin Van Buren forced to migrate from their homes in the southeast section of the United States during the "Trail of Tears" following the Indian Removal Act of 1830. The inhabitants of Isle de Jean Charles escaped the forced march of their peoples and established their own community in Louisiana. Now they must migrate again. The federal government has allocated $48 million to relocate these climate change refugees to the mainland.[2]

Other climate refugees are left to cope on their own. Journalist Christian Parenti met Jose Ramirez on the south bank of the Rio Grande River waiting to cross. Ramirez, a fisherman from the Mexican state of Michoacan, had become an environmental refugee when a "red tide" of toxic algae blooms drove the fish away from the region where he fishes. Human impact on the environment in the form of

---

1. The scientific evidence for climate change is documented by the Intergovernmental Panel on Climate Change, "Climate Change 2014: Synthesis Report," *http://www.ipcc.ch/report/ar5/syr*. See Jacqueline Ashby and Douglas Pachico, "Climate Change: From Concepts to Action," Catholic Relief Services, 2012, *www.crs.org/sites/default/files/tools-research/climate-change-from-concepts-to-action.pdf*.

2. Coral Davenport and Campbell Robertson, "Resettling the First American 'Climate Refugees,'" *New York Times* (May 3, 2016), *www.nytimes.com/2016/05/03/us/resettling-the-first-american-climate-refugees.html?_r=1*.

sewage from tourist hotels and runoff from fertilizers used on Mexican golf courses and farms played a big part in creating the red tide. Poverty and a human-induced environmental disaster converged, leaving Jose little choice but to head north.[3]

The term *refugees* in the chapter title is in quotation marks because historically *refugees* has had a specific, limited meaning in international law. The United Nations 1951 Convention on the Status of Refugees and the 1967 Protocol require states to provide asylum for individuals who are fleeing war or political persecution—for example, current refugees from Syria. To date, there is no UN convention requiring nations to accept those who migrate because climate change makes it impossible to survive where they live, as is the case with Jose Ramirez. "Migration—whether permanent or temporary, internal or international—has always been a possible adaptation for people facing environmental changes."[4] While estimates vary wildly, the International Organization for Migration forecasts that 200 million people will be internally displaced or will migrate to another country by 2050 due to climate change.[5] Try to imagine a population equal to nearly two-thirds of all U.S. citizens forced to leave their homes. Across the globe, both pastoralists and farmers are well attuned to shifting weather patterns. They quickly adjust to those shifts by migrating to cities in times of drought and returning to the countryside when the rains finally come.[6] A Mexican farmer puts it bluntly: "My grandfather, father and I have worked these lands. But now times have changed . . . the rain is coming later now, so that we produce less. The only solution is to go away, at least for a while, [to the United States]."[7] These statements demonstrate, as the International Organization for Migration notes, that while some examples of environmental migration seem clearly forced

---

3. Christian Parenti, *Tropic of Chaos: Climate Change and the New Geography of Violence* (New York: Nation Books, 201), 183–84.

4. Koko Warner, Charles Ehrhart, Alex de Sherbinin, Susanna Adamo, and Tricia Chai-Onn, "In Search of Shelter: Mapping the Effects of Climate Change on Human Migration and Displacement," May 2009, 1, *www.ciesin.columbia.edu/documents/clim-migr-report-june09_media.pdf*.

5. Ibid., 2; see also the International Organization for Migration, "Migration, Climate Change and the Environment: A Complex Nexus," *www.iom.int/complex-nexus*.

6. Warner et al., "In Search of Shelter," 10.

7. Ibid., 7.

and others arise from proactive decisions, there is a wide grey zone between these two poles.[8] While the case of the inhabitants of the Isle de Jean Charles illustrates the first pole and the case of Africans who migrate back and forth between country and city without waiting for disaster to hit illustrates the proactive pole, most climate change refugees fall somewhere in-between.

In many poor countries or regions, internal displacement due to climate change can put a great deal of pressure on the ecosystems and the communities to which migrants flock. This can cause a cascading effect. For example, in the northwest of Kenya, rival ethnic groups fight over access to water holes for their herds or raid their enemies' cattle to replenish stocks that have died off. Sometimes the sporadic clashes break out into full-scale battles. "Climate change," argues Parenti, a journalist who has studied the impact of climate change in the world's conflict zones, "arrives in a world primed for crisis. The current and impending dislocations of climate change intersect with the existing crises of poverty and violence. I call this collision of political, economic, and environmental disasters 'the catastrophic convergence.'"[9] The Pentagon views climate change as a threat multiplier that, combined with other factors, can turn micro battles over, for example, access to water into much larger conflicts. The military approach to this threat multiplier is to reinforce "fortress America" or create what Parenti calls an "armed lifeboat," when what is really needed in the case of Kenya are more wells.[10]

Lifeboat Ethics

Philosopher Garrett Hardin popularized the term "lifeboat ethics" in explicit contrast to environmentalists' use of the term "spaceship Earth." A spaceship implies a captain who gives orders

continued

---

8. International Organization for Migration, "Migration, Climate Change, and the Environment."

9. Parenti, *Tropic of Chaos*, 7.

10. Ibid., 16, 20, 52.

Lifeboat Ethics continued

and others who follow, combined with a stable population and an equality of shared and carefully controlled resources. Hardin notes that none of these conditions is present in the evolving ecological crisis. Instead, the world is sharply divided between the relatively few rich nations and the many poor nations. The rich nations of the world are lifeboats with limited capacity. The vast numbers of poor people are adrift in a sea of chaos. If a rich nation were to haul even a small portion of the poor on board, the boat would swamp and all the people would perish. Hardin developed his theory before climate change was fully grasped, but he might argue that it represents a huge wave that threatens even a well-provisioned lifeboat. To take on board even a small fraction of the potentially 200 million dislocated people by 2050 would sink all of the lifeboats. Those on the lifeboats respond by arming their boats to guard against "boarding parties."[11]

What is your response to Hardin's argument for lifeboat ethics? What assumptions are embedded in the lifeboat metaphor? Are these assumptions valid in your judgment?

Catholic Relief Services (CRS) follows an integral human development model. CRS's model is based on the premise that both individuals and communities possess natural, physical, financial, social, political, and spiritual resources that can be enhanced.[12] Poor people and nations are not flailing around in a turbulent sea. Nor are they merely victims of calamities. They are also not significantly different from people who are not poor and could easily find themselves needing help from others. A social science term for CRS's approach in the field is "asset-based community development." Assets crucial to livelihood can be diversified: water resources can be managed better; soils can be enriched organically; drought-resistant seeds and crops can be introduced.[13]

---

11. Garrett Hardin, "Lifeboat Ethics: The Case against Helping the Poor," *Psychology Today* (September 1974), *www.garretthardinsociety.org/articles/art_lifeboat_ethics_case_against_helping_poor.html*.

12. For a fuller discussion of integral human development, see chapter 7.

13. Ashby and Pachico, "Climate Change," 38, 52–55.

Several principles guide CRS's implementation of its asset-based community development approach: begin with community-level participation; honor local knowledge and skills; recognize social differences; and seek to empower those on the margins. Following these principles builds a community's capacity to respond to unforeseen challenges.[14] The end result is a *resilient* community, one that can build its own lifeboat. "Resilience" is a term used by ecologists to describe the capacity of ecological systems to withstand shocks that would alter their self-organizing and self-sustaining processes. Ecologists use the term "adaptive capacity" to refer to the ability to modify resilience, for example, by introducing elements that strengthen

The Awaradoni

In Ghana, climate change producing rising sea levels has eroded coastal areas. On land, higher temperatures have led to periods of drought coupled with periods of flooding. Villagers dependent on

subsistence agriculture have become vulnerable and, in some cases, displaced. A CRS savings program has helped the women in Awaradoni villages develop businesses that lessen their dependence on subsistence agriculture. For example, some women make shea-nut butter for beauty products from drought-resistant trees. Awaradoni women also collaborate on a basket-weaving business,

Awaradoni weaving baskets

which provides income not dependent on farming, empowers them, and builds community. Adaptation and diversification may enable the Awaradoni to stay in place and thrive in a changed climate.[15]

---

14. Ibid., 58.

15. "Rising above Climate Change in Ghana," Catholic Relief Services, *www.crs.org/stories/rising-above-climate-change-ghana.*

biodiversity.[16] Those who study the impact of climate change on human communities and those, like CRS, who work with communities vulnerable to climate change also follow this basic guiding principle: "Invest in resilience: Increase people's resilience to the impacts of climate change so that fewer are forced to migrate."[17]

As mentioned, climate change refugees are not protected by legally binding, international conventions. In response, the five authors of the report "In Search of Shelter: Mapping the Effects of Climate Change on Human Migration and Displacement" argue that nations should agree to "integrate climate change into existing international and national frameworks for dealing with displacement and migration."[18] However, there are several thorny issues that must be faced and resolved in this process. First, in cases of war or political persecution relocation may be temporary, with return to one's homeland at least a possibility. But the changes wrought by climate change, as seen with Isle de Jean Charles, will be either permanent or last for a century or more. Second, a large grey zone exists between forced and voluntary migration in the case of climate refugees. A generous set of international guidelines must tilt in favor of the vulnerable parties, that is, the migrants. Finally, it is clear, especially in light of the Syrian refugee crisis, that the United Nations High Commissioner for Refugees and nongovernmental organizations that partner with it are stretched beyond their limits in dealing with "traditional" refugees and internally displaced peoples. Their resources must be drastically augmented.[19] The time to gear up is now, not when millions of people find their livelihoods severely compromised by climate change.

The Case of Coffee

In 1982, Carlos Cano became a refugee. In the midst of a civil war and brutal military repression in Guatemala, Cano's father moved his family to Chiapas, Mexico. They stayed for sixteen

---

16. Lance H. Gunderson, "Ecological Resilience in Theory and Application," *Annual Review of Ecology and Systematics*, 31 (November 2000): 425–39.

17. Warner et al., "In Search of Shelter," v.

18. Warner et al., "In Search of Shelter," v.

19. Ibid.

© Philip Laubner / CRS

Carlos Cano shows the coffee leaf rust decimating coffee farms in Guatemala.

years. Peace accords awarded returning refugees acreage in mountainous coffee-growing regions. These families started from scratch but eventually built viable coffee farms. In 2012, however, Carlos became a migrant once again, leaving his home to find work in Mexico. Why? The culprit this time was not civil war, but a fungus: coffee leaf rust.

In 2012, some Guatemalan growers lost 85 percent of their coffee crops. The spread of the fungus, which is directly related to climate change, affects coffee-growing regions across Central America. As temperatures climb, the range of the fungus moves up the mountains, jeopardizing coffee crops at ever-higher elevations.

Because of the work of CRS, Carlos was only a temporary climate refugee. Through a "Green Coffee project," CRS fieldworkers meet with growers to explain what is going on and then to work with them to create solutions. Some growers have introduced new crops like macadamia beans and avocados; others are supplementing their incomes by raising bees. CRS introduces new farming techniques to enrich the soil and encourages the replacement of old coffee trees with fungus-resistant trees. Change has not been easy. "But we have done it," says coffee grower Jose Luis Mateo Mendoza. "We have encouraged ourselves." Back in Guatemala, Carlos agrees. "Despite how difficult the situation has been to get back on our feet, coffee has been the most important thing for us. And it is something . . . we have to keep working at."

Reflect and Discuss

1. Read the Ecowatch report on Isle de Jean Charles ("Louisiana's Vanishing Island: America's First Climate Refugees," Ecowatch, *www.ecowatch.com/louisianas-vanishing-island-americas-first -climate-refugees-1896561560.html*) and view the accompanying MSNBC report ("The Vanishing Island," time: 0:06:22). How does this case enhance your understanding of the impact of climate change on humans? What did you learn from the case of Jose Ramirez? Providing sewage treatment and shifting away from chemical fertilizers is a long-term strategy. What sort of short-term strategies would help environmentally dislocated people like Jose Ramirez?

2. Compare and contrast CRS's use of an asset-based community development approach with Hardin's lifeboat ethics. What sort of ethical concepts are implied in the way that CRS acts in the field?

3. Read the full story of CRS's work with coffee growers in Guatemala along with interviews of Carlos and Jose Luis: Rebekah Kates Lemke, "Moving Up the Mountain: Coffee Farmers Fight against Climate Change" (*www.crs.org/stories /climate-change-guatemala-coffee-leaf-rust*). How does the work of CRS with coffee growers in Guatemala illustrate the principle of resilience? Compare the case of coffee with Hardin's vision of a few lifeboats in a sea of chaos.

CHAPTER 3

Unauthorized Migration to the United States

Josseline Jamileth Hernandez Quinteros was fourteen when she died crossing the Arizona desert, after traveling north from El Salvador through the entire length of Mexico. When Josseline fell sick and could not keep up with the group, she was left behind. Josseline hardly fits the stereotype of an "illegal alien." What was her crime? She wanted to be with her mother, as most children do, and her mother was working in the shadow economy of Los Angeles.[1]

A memorial cross and photos showing Josseline Jamileth Hernandez Quinteros as a young teenager. Like many migrants, she first made a devotion to Mary, the Mother of Jesus, before departing El Salvador for the United States. She died crossing the Arizona desert.

---

1. Margaret Reagan, *The Death of Josseline: Immigration Stories from the Arizona-Mexican Borderlands.* (Boston: Beacon, 2010), xi–xx.

Persons who wear glasses or contact lenses have to have regular vision checks and new lenses from time to time; otherwise, they may become accustomed to dulled or distorted vision. Understanding economic migration is similar. Americans tend to view unauthorized migration through defective lenses. A common (mis)interpretation "sees" unauthorized migration as criminal behavior. Migrants are viewed as being here illegally in order to take something (jobs, welfare benefits, opportunities for education) that belongs to U.S. citizens. This claim of criminality ignores the fact that unauthorized migration is a civil, not a criminal, offense.[2] Moreover, FBI data shows that immigrants are less likely than native-born Americans to commit criminal offenses.

A second theory sees migrants as rational agents who use a cost-benefit analysis in pursuit of their self-interest. Significant wage discrepancies between jobs in one's home country and jobs in the United States make the risks and sorrows of leaving home a smart choice. In this theory, while unauthorized migrants are not to be blamed for their actions, U.S. citizens have no responsibilities or obligations toward them. Owners of large farms may, out of self-interest, hire unauthorized migrants at low wages to provide U.S. citizens with inexpensive fruits and vegetables, but they are not obligated to do so. In this view, blame for this situation rests on the shoulders of the *sending* country, which has not created adequate economic opportunities for its citizens.

Many people assume that the poorest people from the poorest countries are most likely to migrate, but this is not the case. Migration is most likely from countries undergoing rapid modernization of their economies with accompanying dislocations. Moreover, "push" factors are only one variable. This theory ignores any responsibility on the part of *receiving* countries for aiding and abetting unauthorized migration through the receiving countries' labor needs and other factors.

---

2. Parking your car by a fire hydrant, for example, is a civil offense, not a criminal offense. Unauthorized entry into the United States is subject to deportation, not imprisonment. However, under a program called "Operation Streamline," hundreds of migrants each day are prosecuted for illegal entry, a misdemeanor. If they try to reenter after they are deported, they can be charged with a more serious offense. See Joshua Breisblatt, "Operation Streamline: Ten Years of Criminalizing Immigrants," American Immigration Council, *http://immigrationimpact.com/2015/12/15/operation-streamline-immigration/*.

The authors of this book have had many conversations with Mexicans headed north as migrants to the United States; invariably the migrants explained that they were going to the United States to support their families. A family member working in a developed country and sending money back home constitutes a family-based development strategy in economies where there are high levels of unemployment or where ordinary people lack access to home or business loans. While the family loyalty and entrepreneurial spirit of the migrants may be admirable, this perspective, like the second theory, places responsibility on the migrant and the sending country. Given a strong demand by these industries for low wage labor, authorizing this labor makes rational sense.

A fourth theory, the "segmented-labor theory," focuses on the role of the receiving countries. It argues that industrialized economies have a two-tiered labor market: an upper tier that offers good wages and benefits with opportunities for advancement to an educated, highly skilled workforce, and a lower tier with poor wages, little or no benefits, and dead-end jobs for unskilled laborers. In a developed country, well-educated citizens compete for entry into the upper tier, leaving the hard, dirty jobs to a foreign-born labor force. While politicians rail against the "foreign invasion," the agriculture, construction, and hospitality industries, among others, represent a constant "pull" factor.

This fourth theory shows that those who aspire to work in the upper tier benefit from the work of those on the lower tier and, therefore, have some moral obligation for securing their well-being. The pull factors in the United States have been working for a long time; as a consequence migrants have developed their own social networks within the receiving country that make it much easier for new generations of migrants to find a foothold there.

Finally, a fifth theory, the "world-systems theory," emphasizes that migration takes place in a context of global inequality. Globalization has set in motion capital, goods, services, technologies, ideas, and information. These things crisscross national boundaries more than ever before. In this process, the economies of less-developed nations undergo significant dislocations, undermining traditional subsistence occupations. Whole classes of people lose out to the forces of change. The institutions that shape the global economy—the World Bank, the International Monetary Fund, the

World Trade Organization—under the guise of "free trade," have placed the domestic economies of the Global South at a competitive disadvantage. Their policies have forced less developed nations to eliminate tariffs that protect homegrown businesses from unfair competition by more developed economies as the price of entry into export markets.[3] According to this theory, it is largely the most developed nations that have engineered an unjust global economy, which is the major force driving economic migration. Unauthorized migrants highlight injustice in the current world order. The risks they take to come to the United States and the exploitation they endure once they arrive testify to the unfair playing field to which they have been condemned.[4]

Each of these theories sheds light on a different dimension of economic migration. A careful social ethics will consider each theory critically. It is possible that all of these theories, except for the first, can be partially true.[5] Individuals and families do employ strategies, including migration, in order to survive and even flourish. Developed nations do appear to have a two-tiered employment structure. And world systems theory does bring to light the severely skewed playing field produced by globalization.[6] One way to evaluate these theories is to see how they illuminate a particular example of the global economy: the case of corn.

The Case of Corn

In the marketplace of Teotitlan del Valle, a small village in the southern Mexican state of Oaxaca, Josh Healey, a reporter, looks around and asks a native, Carla Moreno, "Where are all the men?" "*Fueron al Norte. . . .* They went north to the U.S.," she replies. "I couldn't believe it," Josh reflects. "Migration seemed to have hit Teotitlan like a plague. . . . How was this possible?"[7]

---

3. On the impact of these international agencies, see "Life and Debt: A Film by Stephanie Black," *http://www.lifeanddebt.org/*.

4. Tisha M. Rajendra, "Justice Not Benevolence: Catholic Social Thought, Migration Theory and the Rights of Migrants," *Political Theology* 15, no. 4 (July 2014): 290–306.

5. Chapter 4 responds to those holding the first theory.

6. Douglas Massey, Jorge Durand, and Nolan J. Malone, *Beyond Smoke and Mirrors: Mexican Immigration in an Era of Economic Integration* (New York: Russel Sage Foundation, 2003), 21–23.

7. Josh Healey, "NAFTA Corn Fuels Immigration," *The Progressive* (April 2013): 22.

"Recent corn sales to Mexico are a bright spot" in the U.S. grain export picture, an online newsletter for agribusiness reports. Sales are up 22 percent from the 2014–2015 marketing period.[8]

"They say we should grow broccoli and asparagus, but where is the training program," a displaced Mexican corn farmer asks. "Do they expect us to take on new methods, invest in new tools, and then suddenly find a new market for our goods?"[9]

"Trade gains are broad and trade pains are very specific. A few people feel the pain, lose jobs, and are displaced," argues Tim Kane of the Heritage Foundation. "That's what Mexico is experiencing. That's the path to progress."[10]

Finally, the head of a Mexican corn producers' association argues that more than a devastating transformation of the Mexican agriculture economy is at stake. "Corn is identity," Enrique Perez says. "We cannot think of Mexican history without corn."[11]

Despite their different outlooks, these examples point to three common things: (1) the impact of globalization on the Mexican agricultural economy, (2) the pressure this creates to migrate, and (3) the centrality of corn in this discussion. Corn has been grown in Mesoamerica for nine thousand years, co-evolving with human beings. In the ancient Mayan genesis narrative, God created humans from corn. In Oaxaca alone, 85,000 varieties of corn are grown, a vital treasury of genetic diversity. But now, the 90 percent of corn growers who farm small plots of land in Mexico have been overwhelmed by huge shipments of corn grown in the United States. One-and-a-half million Mexican farmers have been forced off the land. They have had to migrate either to large Mexican cities or to the United States.[12]

How did this happen? Some theories of migration place the blame on the underdevelopment of the sending country—Mexican

8. "Corn Sales to Mexico Boom: Other Areas Sluggish," *Southwestpress.com* (January 7, 2016): 16.

9. As quoted in Monica Campbell and Tyche Hendricks, "Mexican Corn Farmers See Their Livelihoods Wither Away," *San Francisco Chronicle* (July 31, 2006).

10. As quoted in ibid.

11. Lorne Matalon, "Mexico's Corn Farmers," *PRI's the World* (January 15, 2008), *http://lornematalon.com/2008/01/15/mexico%E2%80%99s-corn-farmers/*.

12. Peter Canby, "Retreat to Subsistence," *The Nation* (July 5, 2010): 30–31; Michael Pollan, "A Flood of US Corn Rips at the Heart of Mexican Farms," *The Ecologist* (June 2004): 6–7.

farmers are clearly at a technological disadvantage compared with large-scale American agribusiness. But in the case of Mexican corn, it is clear that other factors were in play. Specifically, the North American Free Trade Agreement (NAFTA) played a significant role in the decimation of traditional subsistence farming. NAFTA required a phaseout of tariffs that protected corn farmers. "Experts" assumed that Mexican farmers would switch to raising vegetables and fruits that are more labor intensive, giving them a competitive edge.[13]

Corn from U.S. farms soon flooded the Mexican markets and the price farmers received for corn plummeted. But the U.S. edge in industrial farming was not the only reason for U.S. farmers' success. The United States provides more than $10 billion per year in farm subsidies. In 2003, U.S. corn sold in Mexico for $1.76 per bushel when it actually cost $2.66 per bushel to produce.[14] Government subsidies allowed U.S. farmers to sell corn at a loss while still making a profit. In a very real sense, Mexican farmers were competing not only against gigantic agribusinesses, but also against the American taxpayer.

A subsistence farmer, whose family in the best of times is poor, might ask these questions:

- Where am I going to get the capital to grow tomatoes in a greenhouse with an irrigation system?[15]
- How am I going to get the skills for a totally new way of farming?[16]

Concerned observers, in turn, could advance the see-judge-act process by asking the following questions:

- Do theories that see unauthorized migration as simply an act of lawbreaking on the part of individuals or that place blame on Mexico's shoulders fairly represent the ethical issues at stake?

---

13. Canby, "Retreat to Subsistence," 31–32.

14. Gisele Henriquez and Raj Patel, "Agricultural Trade Liberalization and Mexico," *Food First Policy Brief* 7 (2003): 10, 24, 30–31.

15. Anjali Browning, "Corn, Tomatoes, and a Dead Dog: Mexican Agricultural Restructuring after NAFTA and Rural Responses to Declining Maize Production in Oaxaca Mexico," *Mexican Studies/Estudios Mexicanos* 29, no.1 (Winter 2013): 85–119.

16. Ibid.

- How should ethical judgments be made regarding unauthorized migration when economic integration is shaping the context in which a Mexican farmer must decide what to do?

In the case of corn, what happens in Oaxaca and at the Arizona/Sonora border is directly linked to what happens in Iowa and Washington, D.C.

A Brief History of Migration to the United States

Putting current events into a larger context through historical analysis illumines recurrent patterns. During its first century of existence, the United States imposed almost no restrictions on immigration. There was no distinction between legal and illegal immigration. The Anglo-Saxon majority, however, treated many newcomers with hostility. This gave rise to a series of movements called *nativism*.

Nativism

Nativism involves the stereotyping of recent immigrant groups and hostility toward them as a threat to a culture's identity and well-being. Nativism has been a persistent strain in American culture and politics. In 1753, Benjamin Franklin wrote about German immigrants, "Few of their children in the country learn English. . . . The signs in our streets have inscriptions in both languages. . . . Unless the stream of their importation could be turned, they will soon outnumber us and all the advantages we have will not be able to preserve our language, and even our government will become precarious."[17] Note the similarity of Franklin's concerns with stereotypes and fears articulated today by those who see an urgent need to curb immigration.

In 1882 Congress passed the Chinese Exclusion Act. To replace the Chinese labor building railroads in the Southwest, Mexicans were hired.

---

17. As quoted in Joseph Nevins, *Dying to Live* (San Francisco: City Lights, 2008), 111.

In the aftermath of World War I, Congress feared an "invasion" of Italians and others from Southern and Eastern Europe, including members of "the Hebrew Race" escaping pogroms in Russia. The Johnson-Reed Act of 1924 imposed a quota system based upon the existing proportion of ethnic groups and a racial hierarchy, which was intended to maintain the dominance of those whose ancestors came from Northern Europe. For the first time, the Act established a tiny border patrol to monitor America's borders. It is important to note that the Act placed no restrictions at all on immigration from Latin America in deference to growers in the Southwest who were dependent on Mexican labor.[18]

In fact, until the mid-1980s, a revolving door pattern prevailed regarding the entry of Mexican workers into the United States. During economic boom times and periods of labor shortages, the United States Border Patrol looked the other way as Mexican workers flocked to the fields of California and the Southwest. When the economy contracted, Mexican workers were deported. During the Great Depression of the 1930s, an estimated 400,000 laborers of Mexican ancestry were deported, 60 percent of whom were actually American citizens. The revolving door metaphor suggests that the true purpose of the Border Patrol has been "to regulate the flow of Mexican labor not to prevent it."[19]

During the Second World War, growers facing labor shortages pressed the government to establish the *Bracero* program.[20] This program permitted Mexican workers to work under contract with growers in the Southwest. Under the terms of the contract workers were allowed to stay in the United States only as long as they remained employed with their original employer, who could terminate the contract at will, leading to deportation. This one-sided system led to widespread abuses by the growers, and in the era of the civil rights movement of the 1960s, Congress was pressured to cancel the program.

---

18. Massey et al., *Beyond Smoke and Mirrors*, 24; Mae M. Ngai, *Impossible Subjects: Illegal Aliens and the Making of Modern America* (Princeton: Princeton University Press, 2004), 3, 18, 20–24, 26, 60, 130–32.

19. Timothy Dunn, *The Militarization of the U.S.-Mexico Border, 1978–1992* (Austin: University of Texas at Austin Press, 1996), 162.

20. *Bracero* was the term for a Mexican laborer admitted legally into the United States for seasonal contract work until the *Braceros* program was cancelled.

A new law passed in 1965 gave every nation a quota of twenty thousand immigrants per year. What seems fair on the surface ignored several key facts. The relatively affluent citizens of the nations of Northern Europe had no real need to emigrate in large numbers and the citizens of the poorest nations did not have the means to emigrate. Mexicans, however, not only had historic ties to the Southwest—after all, it had been part of Mexico for much longer than it had been part of the United States—but their labor was in high demand. The law did nothing to address the economic push-pull factors that led many more than twenty thousand Mexicans to seek work in the United States.

The *Bracero* program left three legacies. First, the growers became accustomed to having a low-cost workforce lacking legal protections. They substituted unauthorized migrants for the *braceros*. Second, the migrants themselves developed a pattern of *"circular migration,"* working in the United States according to agricultural seasonal needs and returning to Mexico in the off-season. Even workers in other industries moved back and forth between jobs in *El Norte* and their homes and families in Mexico. Third, some of the *braceros* stayed in the United States and created social networks with their hometowns in Mexico. This facilitated future authorized and unauthorized migration.

Whether this pattern of circular migration is considered just or unjust, Douglas Massey of the Mexican Migration Project argues that it worked. From 1985 on, however, a series of changes in immigration law took "a wrench to a precision clock."[21] Why did the United States not recognize the benefits of labor from Latin America? Why did it not replace the exploitative *Bracero* program with a more just guest worker program? One response might be to acknowledge that nativist hostility recurs in contrast with the American tradition of welcoming hardworking peoples from other lands. But why is there a strong nativist movement today?

Those who have studied the complexities of immigration policy and its underlying politics offer an alternative theory. First, globalization has created dislocations in many economies of developing countries, leading to unprecedented migration within and emigration

---

21. Massey et al., *Beyond Smoke and Mirrors*, 2.

from these countries. This gives rise to fears of an "invasion" from poorer countries, despite evidence that only a small percentage of any nation's populations emigrate, usually only temporarily, as sending countries develop.[22] A good example is Ireland, which experienced more than a century of emigration but then became a receiving country—until the last recession. Second, these fears have become acute, because globalization also dislocates less-skilled workers in affluent countries whose jobs have been outsourced to other countries. This has produced greater social inequality within countries. There is also what noted essayist Barbara Ehrenreich calls a "fear of falling" into the lower tier of the two-tiered economy.[23] Third, the increasing role of international organizations like the World Trade Organization and multilateral treaties like NAFTA create the impression that the nation-state can no longer protect its citizens from economic harm. In this era of dislocation at home as well as abroad and in this atmosphere of fear, politicians have found a convenient scapegoat in unauthorized immigrants. As President Reagan put it, "A nation that cannot control its borders is not a nation."[24] For President Reagan and a host of politicians, clamping down on unauthorized migration across the U.S.-Mexican border became a cure-all for the complex problems of globalization.

In 1994, the Immigration and Naturalization Service developed a new strategic plan, "Prevention through Deterrence."[25] This plan sought to deprive migrants of easy access to the United States through urban gateways. A series of walls were built at key U.S.-Mexico crossings (Tijuana/San Diego, Ciudad Juarez/El Paso,

---

22. Ibid., 143–49; Saskia Sassen, "The Making of Migration," in *Living With(out) Borders: Catholic Theological Ethics and the Migration of Peoples*, ed. Agnes M. Brazal and Maria Theresa Davila (Maryknoll, NY: Orbis, 2016), 15–16. Evidence suggests that the large wave of Mexicans entering the United States has subsided, with more Mexicans returning to Mexico than are coming. See Pew Research Center, "Net Migration from Mexico Falls to Zero—and Perhaps Less," *www.pewhispanic.org/2012/04/23/net-migration-from-mexico-falls-to-zero-and-perhaps-less/*.

23. Barbara Ehrenreich, *Fear of Falling* (New York: Harper Perennial, 1990), 70–71.

24. President Reagan, as quoted in Raymond Michalowski, "Border Militarization and Migrant Suffering," *Social Justice* 34, no. 2 (2007): 70; Joseph Nevins, "Searching for Security: Boundary and Immigration Enforcement in an Age of Intensifying Globalization," *Social Justice* 28, no. 2 (2001): 139–40.

25. Robert Bach, "Transforming Border Security: Prevention First," *Homeland Security Affairs* 1, article 2 (June 2005), *www.hsaj.org/articles/181*.

and Nogales, Sonora/Nogales, Arizona). These walls forced migrants to take dangerous routes through brutal deserts to enter the United States. Walls, as Border Patrol agents attest, are exercises in futility. The Border Patrol has found numerous tunnels under the walls and holes cut through the fences. The number of deaths of migrants increased rapidly as they were forced to make hazardous crossings. But walls did not deter migration, as many risked traveling the "Devil's Highway."[26]

> I met with a woman . . . in Altar [Sonora] one night who had a couple of kids with her and someone in my delegation said, "Don't you understand the risk you're taking? You've got a couple of kids who are just above toddler age and you could die out there." And she looked that woman right in the face and she said, "Look, I have two choices: I can risk everything . . . and maybe win a future for my kids. Or I can stay at home and watch them die a slow death." If that is the choice that these people . . . confront, it doesn't matter what we do at the border to try and stop them. They are going to keep trying to come the same way you would or I would.[27]

In the face of this escalating tragedy, a number of humanitarian organizations were created to save migrants' lives by distributing water bottles along trails frequented by migrants.

The walls also had several unintended consequences. First, because the trip was dangerous and the fees charged by "coyotes" to lead migrants through the desert were exorbitant, the walls put an end to "circular migration." Unauthorized migrants still came, but now they stayed and set down roots in the new country rather than working for a time and then returning home. Second, because circular migration was no longer possible, increasingly migration by whole families became a new pattern, replacing migration mostly by young men.[28]

---

26. See Luis Alberto Urrea, *The Devil's Highway* (New York: Little, Brown and Co., 2004).

27. Interview with Rick Ufford-Chase, "Dying to Get In: Undocumented Immigration at the U.S./Mexico Border," directed by Brett Tolley, *www.youtube.com /watch?v=5QgaGf1ans8*, (time: 0:39:36).

28. Massey et al., *Beyond Smoke and Mirrors*, 131–32.

No More Deaths

No More Deaths is a humanitarian organization founded in 2004 to address the crisis of migrant deaths in the Arizona desert. These deaths—around seven thousand by 2016—were the foreseen consequence of the Border Patrol's "Prevention through Deterrence" strategic plan. Volunteers leave jugs of water in the desert along paths followed by migrants. The water aids migrants who have been incapacitated by the extreme desert heat. Along with other organizations in Mexico, No More Deaths provides food and first aid to migrants deported to Mexico. They bring attention to abuses by Border Patrol officers and violations of basic rights.[29]

Migrants cross desolate, dangerous areas where temperature extremes add to the peril. Volunteers with No More Deaths set water out along the migrant trails.

In the aftermath of 9-11, the Border Patrol was folded into Customs and Border Protection within the Department of Homeland Security. Fears of terrorism rose above the fears produced by globalization. A new strategic plan consciously fused unauthorized migration with the threat of terrorism.[30] Dismissing the idea that "illegal aliens" were simply migrants pursuing the economic benefits of working in the United States, the plan argued that they were a

29. See "No More Deaths: No Mass Muertes," *www.youtube.com/watch?v=8M mOWHHCav4*, (time: 0:06:51).

30. See Customs and Border Protection, "Vision and Strategy, 2020," *www.cbp .gov/sites/default/files/documents/CBP-Vision-Strategy-2020.pdf*; David Bacon, *Illegal People: How Globalization Creates Migration and Criminalizes Immigrants* (Boston: Beacon, 2008), 111.

threat to national security. Congress agreed with this argument and increased the Border Patrol's budget and number of agents astronomically. From 1990 to 2015, the number of Border Patrol agents grew by 500 percent, from around 4,000 to 20,273. In the same period, its budget grew from $262,647,000 to $3,797,821,000, an increase of more than 1,400 percent.[31] To put this in context, more is spent on border protection than on the FBI, Drug Enforcement Administration (DEA), Alcohol, Tobacco, Firearms (ATF), Secret Service, U.S. Marshal's Service, and National Park Service combined. Yet politicians still call for added border security as a condition for immigration reform.

Throughout this process, unauthorized migrants, now well established in American communities, have not been silent or passive. In April 2006, massive demonstrations of Latino immigrants and their supporters sprang up in American cities calling for comprehensive immigration reform. Among them were young people carrying signs saying, "We Have a Dream Too," echoing Dr. Martin Luther King Jr.'s famous speech. These demonstrators, approximately 1.8 million immigrants, were brought here as children. They are known as the DREAMers, named for a bill that has been repeatedly introduced in Congress but never passed by both Houses.[32] "We were brought to the United States by our families when we were young," one group of DREAMers declared. "This is the only country we have known as home. We have the same hopes and dreams as other young people, and have worked hard to excel at school and contribute to our communities. But because of our immigration status, we've spent our childhoods in fear and hiding, unable to achieve our full potential."

---

31. Border Patrol staffing, *https://www.cbp.gov/sites/default/files/assets/documents/2016-Oct/BP%20Staffing%20FY1992-FY2016.pdf*; Border Patrol budget history, *https://www.cbp.gov/sites/default/files/assets/documents/2016-Oct/BP%20Budget%20History%201990-2016.pdf*.

32. The Development, Relief and Education for Alien Minors (DREAM) Act provides an opportunity for unauthorized migrants who were brought to the United States as minors to gain permanent resident status provided they have enrolled in college or have served in the military. See American Immigration Council, "A Comparison of the Dream Act and Other Proposals for Undocumented Youth," June 5, 2012, *www.americanimmigrationcouncil.org/research/comparison-dream-act-and-other-proposals-undocumented-youth*.

Paradoxically, the DREAMers embody America's core values—commitment to education and hard work, loyalty to family, desire to reach one's "full potential"—yet in the eyes of many Americans, they are criminals, threats to the nation. In 2012, President Obama signed an executive order known as Deferred Action for Childhood Arrivals (DACA), which offered a reprieve from deportation and work permits to some 800,000 DREAMers. But a reprieve is not a solution, nor is an executive order a law.[33] The troubled history of America's treatment of immigrants continues.

Reflect and Discuss

1. Which aspects of America's history of immigration strike you as most important? Which aspects need to be explored more deeply?
2. What values are expressed and what ethical issues are raised by the five quotations that open "The Case of Corn"? How does that case affect how you think ethically about economic migration?
3. What ethical issues does the creation of the "Devil's Highway" raise?
4. What are the arguments, pro and con, regarding legalization of the status of DREAMers?

33. Marie Friedmann Marquardt, "Double Threat: Unauthorized Migration as a Global Phenomenon," in *Religious and Ethical Perspectives on Global Migration*, ed. Elizabeth Collier and Charles Strain (Lanham, MD: Lexington, 2014), 13–32.

CHAPTER 4

The Current Debate: Restrictionists versus Nonrestrictionists

Migration affects almost every corner of the world. The regions most affected, in terms of numbers of people fleeing violence and extreme poverty, are Africa and the Middle East, challenging countries in those regions to accommodate millions of migrants. People in the United States tend to focus on migrants bound for this country, without realizing that the vast majority of the world's migrants seek entrance to other countries. Even in Latin America, many migrants flee to countries other than the United States. The United States has not experienced a massive influx of desperately needy people comparable to the waves of immigrants that have entered many other countries. For most people reading this book, though, the United States is home, and most people's lives are lived primarily at the local level. For that reason, this chapter focuses on some of the ways migration is viewed in the United States.

Since the beginning of the European colonial expansion to the North American continent, questions about who should be allowed in, for what reasons, and how long they should stay have been hotly debated. The interplay between economics and labor needs, together with beliefs about race, world events, and politics, have all contributed to a mishmash of immigration laws that are more complex than U.S. tax laws.

While opinions on immigration run the gamut from advocating closed borders to supporting open borders, most people currently favor policies that fit into one of two categories: restrictive or nonrestrictive. People favoring restrictive policies tend to believe that immigration negatively impacts the United States. Those favoring nonrestrictive policies tend to believe immigration is a benefit to U.S. society and are likely to support both expanding the allowable reasons for immigration and increasing caps on the number of people permitted to immigrate.[1]

This chapter examines some prominent restrictionist assertions and proposals, arranged under three headings: "They [immigrants] Steal Our Jobs," "Get in Line," and "Build a Wall."

"They Steal Our Jobs"

This charge concerns how immigration affects the receiving country's economic wellbeing. Most research on economic issues indicates that, overall, immigration benefits the U.S. economy.[2] As with every other aspect of immigration, economic impacts are complex. Many mainstream assumptions about these factors contradict research findings. For example, many people are surprised to learn that 46 percent of immigrants have white-collar jobs and at least some college education.[3]

Restrictionists fear that increased immigration means higher unemployment for U.S. citizens due to labor competition, lower wages for citizens who remain employed in industries where immigrants are employed, and a decrease in the quality of working conditions.

---

1. For a detailed treatment of the arguments for and against immigration, see Elizabeth Collier, "Arguing about Immigration: The Claims of Restrictionists and Non-Restrictionists," in *Religious and Ethical Perspectives on Global Migration*, ed. Elizabeth W. Collier and Charles R. Strain (Lanham, MD: Lexington, 2014), 229–55. See also Aviva Chomsky, *"They Take Our Jobs!" and Twenty Other Myths about Immigration* (Boston: Beacon, 2007).

2. Information in this chapter comes from a wide range of researchers and organizations. In contrast, restrictionist and anti-immigrant publications tend to cite the same few sources: George Borjas, Mark Krikorian, Citizen and Immigration Services (CIS), and Federation for American Immigration Reform (FAIR). Some of the citations in this chapter can be read for further information on researcher critiques of Borjas' and Krikorian's research methods and interpretations of data.

3. Daniel Costa, David Cooper, and Heidi Shierholz, "Facts about Immigration and the U.S. Economy," Economic Policy Institute, August 12, 2014, *www.epi.org /publication/immigration-facts/*.

They argue that although the United States needed immigrant labor for building infrastructure and for manufacturing in the past, today this country does not need foreign workers. Restrictionists think that low-skilled citizen workers have fewer job options if there is a large or continuous influx of immigrant labor. Restrictionists also believe that increases in highly skilled foreign workers who qualify for the H-1B visa[4] depress wages in those areas, thereby dissuading U.S. university students from pursuing those careers and prompting industries to cyclically import cheap legal foreign labor.

The reality is complex and can vary from one region to another, from cities to smaller communities, from one job category to another, and from one state's legal framework to another's. Each element needs to be studied carefully. Most studies, by a wide range of organizations and researchers, report that immigration overall provides a net economic and employment benefit.

Lower-skilled immigrants are often employed in jobs that do not attract native-born citizens.[5] Interestingly, the types of work lower-skilled immigrants do and that of their lower-skilled native-born counterparts complement each other.[6] A study of workers in the state of Georgia, for instance, found that an increase of undocumented workers resulted in a small increase in the wages of native-born workers because of their increased productivity.[7] Nationwide, 10 percent of workers who are employed by privately owned businesses

---

4. H-1B visas are used by employers who have job openings for positions that require at least a bachelor's degree. These visas are good for three years and are renewable for one additional three-year period. Companies must file applications and pay fees for each case to be reviewed. H-1B visas are capped at 85,000 per year.

5. H-2A visas are for seasonal agricultural workers. Although there are no caps for these visas, employers must demonstrate a need that cannot be filled by domestic laborers. H-2B, for nonagricultural workers, caps at 66,000 annually. After three years, a worker is restricted from entry for a period of time before a new visa can be issued. See "H-2A Temporary Agriculture Workers," U.S. Citizenship and Immigration Services, *www.uscis.gov/working-united-states/temporary-workers/h-2a-temporary-agricultural-workers*, and "H-2B Temporary Non-Agricultural Workers," U.S. Citizenship and Immigration Services, *www.uscis.gov/working-united-states/temporary-workers/h-2b-temporary-non-agricultural-workers*.

6. Julie L. Hotchkiss, Myriam Quispe-Agnoli, and Fernando Rios-Avila, "The Wage Impact of Undocumented Workers: Evidence from Administrative Data," *Southern Economic Journal* 81, no. 4 (April 2015): 874–906.

7. Ibid.

are employed by a company owned by an immigrant. Those immigrant-owned businesses pay out $126 billion in payroll.[8] Immigrants themselves are more likely to start a small business than native-born citizens. While native-born small business openings have declined in recent years, immigrant small business ownership has grown. Immigrants accounted for 28 percent of small businesses opened in 2011, even though immigrants only accounted for 12.9 percent of the overall population.[9] Researchers looking at how many jobs are created by the existence of immigrants have found evidence that between 1980 and 2000, each immigrant present resulted in the creation of 1.2 jobs, which seemed to go to native workers. That means that for every one thousand immigrants, approximately 1,200 jobs are created that go to citizen workers. Overall, it appears that local workers benefit from the arrival of more immigrants.[10]

Immigrants have started 25 percent of the businesses in seven of the eight fastest growing sectors.[11] Google, Sun Microsystems, and eBay are among the major companies started by immigrants. This is where future job growth will occur. In California, while immigrants are 27.2 percent of the state's population, they own 36.6 percent of all businesses and start 44.6 percent of all new businesses.[12] Similar findings have been published for those states with the largest volume of immigrants: Texas, Illinois, Florida, New York, New Jersey, Arizona, and Georgia. Soon after the institution of President Trump's January 27, 2017, travel ban, affecting people from Iraq, Syria, Iran, Sudan, Libya, Somalia, and Yemen, one hundred companies signed a legal brief explaining that restricting immigration in general or creating unexpected travel restraints will prompt high-performing, job-creating companies to open offices or

---

8. The Partnership for a New American Economy, "Open for Business: How Immigrants Are Driving Small Business Creation in the United States," August 2012, *www.renewoureconomy.org/research/open-for-business-how-immigrants-are-driving-small-business-creation-in-the-united-states-2/*.

9. Ibid.

10. Gihoon Hong and John McLaren, "Are Immigrants a Shot in the Arm for the Local Economy?" NBER Working Paper 21123, April 2015, National Bureau of Economic Research, *www.nber.org/papers/w21123*.

11. The Partnership for a New American Economy, "Open for Business."

12. Ibid.

fully relocate overseas, where their employees will not have travel concerns and where these companies can hire the best talent worldwide. The legal brief also pointed out that two hundred of the Fortune 500 companies were started by immigrants or their children. Signatories included Facebook, Twitter, Intel, EBay, Netflix, Uber, Levi Strauss, and Chobani.[13]

An Immigrant Entrepreneur

Alex Torrenegra first saw a computer when he was four years old and living in Colombia. At fourteen he owned one. By age nineteen, Alex employed twenty workers in a high tech business. Alex and his family fled violence in Colombia in 1998, and Alex started over in the United States. He became a "serial entrepreneur," creating a dozen companies that today do $35 million in business per year.[14]

In addition to business creation, immigrants are also involved in many of the innovations in the United States. In 2011, a widely cited study reported that 76 percent of the patents awarded to the top ten patent-producing U.S. universities had at least one foreign-born inventor. They came from eighty-eight different countries. Many of their inventions contributed to cutting-edge fields.[15] In 2008, the National Bureau of Economic Research looked at state and federal data to determine the effect of immigration on patents. It estimated that with a 1 percent increase in immigrants graduating from U.S. universities, there is a 15 percent per capita rise in patents.[16] World

---

13. "U.S. Tech Titans Lead Legal Brief against Trump Travel Ban," Reuters, Technology News (February 6, 2017), www.reuters.com/article/us-usa-trump-immigration-tech-idUSKBN15L0IY.

14. Ibid.

15. The Partnership for a New American Economy, "Patent Pending: How Immigrants are Reinventing the American Economy," June 2012, www.renewoureconomy.org/wp-content/uploads/2013/07/patent-pending.pdf.

16. Jennifer Hunt and Marjolaine Gauthier-Loiselle, "How Much Does Immigration Boost Innovation?" NBER Working Paper 14312, September 2008, National Bureau of Economic Research, www.nber.org/papers/w14312.

Bank researchers found that "both international graduate students and skilled immigrants have a significant and positive impact on future patent applications. . . . Thus reductions in foreign graduate students from visa restrictions could significantly reduce U.S. innovative activity."[17] In 2016, all six Nobel Prize winners in the United States in economics and science fields were immigrants.[18]

Immigrants' contributions to the U.S. economy extend beyond wages, employment, entrepreneurship, and innovation. One example is the U.S. housing market, a significant contributor to the overall economy. In the last twenty years, immigrants have been responsible for 27.5 percent of U.S. household growth and, for people under age forty-five, they account for almost all of the household growth.[19] Some analysts argue that immigrants are actually propping up the market because of the lower numbers of people in Generation X and lower homeownership rates of millenials.[20] Homeownership contributes to economic activity and profits through banks, mortgage companies, realtors, new construction, and home improvements.

Immigrants present in the United States contribute at the local, state, and federal levels through their taxes as well. They pay local sales taxes, property taxes through rent or homeownership, and taxes on their income. It is estimated that 75 percent of undocumented immigrants pay into the federal tax system, but due to their status, are never able to recoup those payments because they are not eligible for Social Security. In 2005, it was estimated that undocumented workers paid $7 billion into Social Security and $1.5 billion into Medicare.[21] Stephen C. Goss, the head actuary at the Social Security

---

17. Gnanaraj Chellaraj, Keith E. Maskus, and Aaditya Mattoo, "The Contribution of Skilled Immigration and International Graduate Students to U.S. Innovation," World Bank Policy Research Paper 3588, May 2005, *papers.ssrn.com/sol3/papers .cfm?abstract_id=744625.*

18. Stewart Anderson, "Immigrants Flooding America with Nobel Prizes," *Forbes*, October 16, 2016, *www.forbes.com/sites/stuartanderson/2016/10/16/immigrants -flooding-america-with-nobel-prizes/#214f4b2b7f5f.*

19. Gillian B. White, "Can Immigrants Save the Housing Market?" *Atlantic* (January 8, 2015) *www.theatlantic.com/business/archive/2015/01/can-immigrants -save-the-housing-market/384332/.*

20. Ibid.

21. Eduardo Porter, "Illegal Immigrants Are Bolstering Social Security with Billions," *New York Times*, Business Section, April 5, 2005.

Administration, estimated that the funding deficit in Social Security would be 10 percent higher without the contributions of people working with others' Social Security numbers.[22]

At the federal level, legal and undocumented immigration both result in a net economic benefit. People who immigrate legally must prove that they will not become a public charge. If they are not already employed in the United States and are not independently wealthy, then those petitioning for them must show that they make enough to support the immigrant if necessary. While legal immigrants can access public benefits in a few ways, a National Academy of Science study "found that the typical immigrant and his or her offspring will pay a net $80,000 more in taxes during their lifetime than they collect in government services." If immigrant and offspring have a college degree, that amount goes up to $198,000.[23] Undocumented immigrants are not eligible for public benefits.

While immigration is a net benefit, there are also costs, which largely fall on local communities with large numbers of recently arrived undocumented immigrants. These costs tend to be for public education of children, hospital systems that absorb the costs of serving people without insurance or Medicaid, and the state criminal justice system when the government detains undocumented immigrants. Some local communities have sued the federal government to recoup costs associated with these issues, since the economic benefits at the federal level are not often shifted to local communities to offset such costs.

"Get in Line"

This comment is aimed at undocumented immigrants, telling them that if they want to immigrate to the United States they should go through legal channels. To those who say that their ancestors came here legally it must be noted that if they came in the mid-nineteenth

---

22. Ibid.

23. Daniel Griswold, "Immigrants Have Enriched American Culture and Enhanced Our Influence in the World," originally published in *Insight*, February 18, 2002, found at *www.cato.org/publications/commentary/immigrants-have-enriched-american-culture-enhanced-our-influence-world*.

century they did not "get in line," because there were no laws regulating immigration. This complaint assumes that there is a "line" to get into and that the line moves within a reasonable time frame.

Family reunification is one priority of U.S. immigration policy. Ideally, spouses and minor children of U.S. citizens should enter the country within a few months of their application. But administrative backlogs are so large that the United States Citizenship and Immigration Services (USCIS) has invented a second form so that qualified applicants can enter and reunite with their family while their application for a green card is being processed.[24] Other relative categories face limits based on their relationship and on country quotas. For example, unmarried adult children of U.S. citizens have a much longer wait time. In September 2016, USCIS was processing applications from Mexican adult children submitted in March 1995 and from Filipino adult children submitted in July 2005. The adult child who marries during the wait period falls into an even lower preference category. If the family member, while waiting, spent even one unauthorized year in the United States, a ten-year penalty would be applied before legal reentry is permitted. Family members have to decide if they are going to wait for the long legal process to complete or reunite with their family member without permission.

For employment-based applications, issues vary depending on the visa. The cap on visas allowed by Congress for nonimmigrant categories is based on political maneuvering instead of the labor needs of actual industries. The H-1B category is the most well-known visa category with this issue.[25] For the past few years, Congress has allowed 65,000 H-1B visas per fiscal year, along with another 20,000 for those immigrants meeting a master's degree requirement.[26] Since 2013, there have been so many applications in the first week that

---

24. For information about this form, see "V Nonimmigrant," United States Citizenship and Immigration Services, *https://www.uscis.gov/green-card/green-card-through -family/green-card-through-special-categories-family/v-nonimmigrant*.

25. For a primer on the challenges employers face, see Zoe Henry, "Everything You Need to Know about the H-1B Visa," *Inc.*, March 2016, *www.inc.com/magazine /201603/zoe-henry/h-1-b-visa-hiring-foreign-employees-breakdown.html*.

26. For some details on this process, see "H-1B Fiscal Year (FY) 2017 Cap Season," USCIS, *www.uscis.gov/working-united-states/temporary-workers/h-1-b-specialty -occupations-and-fashion-models/h-1-b-fiscal-year-fy-2017-cap-season#count*.

new fiscal year numbers are available that the USCIS started a lottery system. In 2015, there were 213,000 applications submitted in just the first seven days of the new fiscal year cycle. Fiscal year 2017 began on October 1, 2016. As of April 2016, applications were no longer being accepted because the numbers of applications already on file well exceeded the annual cap.[27]

Some global companies game the system and receive an outsized number of visas. Some companies open offices overseas, so they can circumvent the system in the United States and hire highly desirable and innovative workers; this practice is detrimental to local communities that would otherwise have the income and sales taxes, homeownership, and other economic contributions of those workers. Some immigrants end up working for U.S. competitors or starting their own companies to compete, since no visas are available. It comes as no surprise that reform of employment-based visas has been the top legislative priority for some U.S. companies, such as Microsoft.

The H-2A visa can be used for several categories of workers, including those in agriculture. Many employers insist, though, that the program does not work for them.[28] The rules allow for the visa to be used for a seasonal worker for one year, with the option of renewing for two more years before a worker must leave the United States for at least six months before the employer can apply for them to return again.[29] This doesn't give a farmer a consistent workforce. As with the economic arguments given above, farm owners argue that low-skill or unskilled immigrant labor creates other related or complementary jobs that native workers fill. In Congressional testimony, statistics from an apple orchard in New York indicated that two hundred Jamaican workers filling positions for eight weeks, twelve

27. Julia Preston, "Large Companies Game H-1B Visa Program, Costing the U.S. Jobs," *New York Times*, November 10, 2015, *www.nytimes.com/2015/11/11/us/large-companies-game-h-1b-visa-program-leaving-smaller-ones-in-the-cold.html*; "USCIS Reaches FY 2017 H-1B Cap," United States Citizenship and Immigration Services, *www.uscis.gov/news/news-releases/uscis-reaches-fy-2017-h-1b-cap*.

28. For the perspective of a California farm owner, see Jennifer Medina, "California Farmers Short of Labor, and Patience," *New York Times*, March 29, 2014, *www.nytimes.com/2014/03/30/us/california-farmers-short-of-labor-and-patience.html*.

29. For details on the restrictions and requirements of the H-2A visa, see "H-2A Temporary Agricultural Program Details," United States Department of Labor, *www.foreignlaborcert.doleta.gov/h_2a_details.cfm*.

working for eight months, and twelve working for five months, created fifty year-round jobs for domestic laborers.[30]

Some restrictionists have succeeded at the state level in instituting punitive measures for being undocumented, but these measures have actually backfired economically. In 2011, Georgia's punitive measures were successful in driving fearful immigrants from the state, but it also left farmers with $140 million in crops rotting in the fields. The following year, when no native workers were found, the state brought in prisoners to do the work.[31] Farmers contend that many agricultural jobs, while low-skill, do require experience and expertise depending on the crop. There is evidence that a continued focus on restrictive immigration policies will move 61 percent of fruit production out of the United States due to labor shortages.[32] These are not isolated examples. There are many stories of crops that may need to be grown outside the United States and existing farms that can't expand due to labor shortages. All of these have multifaceted negative economic consequences for local communities, farmers, and state and federal tax coffers.

The issues highlighted so far show the challenges that family members, workers, and employers face with "the line" for the immigration process. For many people, though, there is no line. For most categories of "the line," a specific employer or family relationship is required. If an actual employer is not aware of specific immigrants and their skills, then those persons will not have access to a qualifying employer to file the appropriate visa. Also, a visa category may not exist for the jobs that an immigrant can or is willing to do, even if there are plenty of employers with unfilled positions. There may be something noncriminal in their immigration history that precludes them from ever being eligible to enter the United States again, such as an unscrupulous notary who filed erroneous paperwork on their behalf.

---

30. Alyson Eastman, "Written Testimony by Alyson Eastmon, President and Owner of Lake Home Business Services, Inc., Dba Book-Ends Associates," U.S. Senate Committee of the Judiciary, April 22, 2013, *www.judiciary.senate.gov/imo/media /doc/04-22-13EastmanTestimony.pdf*.

31. Benjamin Powell, "The Law of Unintended Consequences: Georgia's Immigration Law Backfires," *Forbes.com*, May 17, 2012, *www.forbes.com/sites/real spin/2012/05/17/the-law-of-unintended-consequences-georgias-immigration-law-back-fires/#76bc59ba404a*.

32. Alan Bjerga, "Crops Rot While Trump-Led Immigration Backlash Idles Farm Work," *Bloomberg Politics*, June 6, 2016, *www.bloomberg.com/politics/ articles/2016-06-06/crops-rot-while-trump-led-immigration-backlash-idles-farm-lobby*.

"Build the Wall"

Proponents of a wall contend that it is necessary first to secure the Southern U.S. border—by creating a physical barrier between the United States and Mexico—before work on other immigration reforms can begin. The border that the United States shares with Mexico is roughly two thousand miles long.[33] Proponents of a wall rarely grapple with the feasibility of building a wall or ask if such a wall will be effective—either for stopping migrants from crossing the border or inhibiting the drug trade or human trafficking. There are currently about 650 miles that have some sort of a physical barrier. In planning for a physical barrier, there are environmental concerns, including how the construction and the barrier will affect endangered species, treaty obligations, river flood zones, natural rain runoff routes, private property concerns, existing river-flow areas, and other such issues.[34]

The current barriers are more of a "fence" meant to impede vehicles and pedestrians—not the high concrete wall envisioned by some. In 2009, the estimate for building a simple fence was $2.8–3.9 million per mile in metropolitan areas and $16 million per mile in deserts or mountains.[35] Costs for maintaining the wall varied between $16.9 million and $70 million per mile, depending on location.[36] These estimates do not include video surveillance or Border Patrol costs for monitoring the fence.

Laying aside questions of the feasibility of building and maintaining a fence, would such a barrier be effective? In areas where a fence exists, drug smugglers and traffickers dig tunnels. While the border patrol can search along the border for such tunnels, there is no technology that can detect the digging or existence of

33. James Whitlow Delano, "This Is What the U.S.-Mexico Border Wall Actually Looks Like," *National Geographic*, *http://news.nationalgeographic.com/2016/03/160304-us-mexico-border-fence-wall-photos-immigration/*.

34. Tribune News Services, "Trump Wants to Build a Wall on the U.S.-Mexico Border. Can It Be Done?" *Chicago Tribune*, March 8, 2016, *www.chicagotribune.com/news/nationworld/ct-trump-wall-mexico-20160308-story.html*.

35. Glen Kessler, "Trump's Dubious Claim That His Border Wall Would Cost $8 Billion," *Washington Post*, February 11, 2016, *www.washingtonpost.com/news/fact-checker/wp/2016/02/11/trumps-dubious-claim-that-his-border-wall-would-cost-8-billion/*.

36. Ibid.

tunnels. In some places, there are so many tunnels that the ground is described as "Swiss cheese."[37] When a new fence is built, smugglers and migrants change routes to those that are in desolate desert or ranchland areas. As discussed in the introduction, these areas are more dangerous for migrants, and they don't seem to deter the criminal activity of drug gangs and human traffickers. People who cannot meet their basic needs are going to find ways to enter the United States, no matter how dangerous.

© Jonathan McIntosh via Flickr

On the Nogales, Sonora, Mexico, side of the wall, crosses symbolize migrants who have died crossing the Arizona desert.

When migration flows decrease along the border, it is usually due to an economic downturn, as happened during the Great Recession in the late 2000s and the resulting employment opportunity decrease, not a new section of fence being erected.

Policy changes between the late 1950s and late 1970s reduced the number of guest worker visas available to Mexicans from 450,000 to zero and the number of resident visas for Mexicans from virtually unlimited to 20,000 per year.[38] Labor demand, however, remained high. As mentioned in chapter 3, a pattern of "circular migration" prevailed, even among unauthorized migrants, after the end of the *Bracero* program. Heightened border enforcement, including the building of current barriers in the early 1990s, changed that pattern to one of permanent settlement. As workers decided to remain because of border enforcement, their families began migrating. Between 1986 and 2008, the number of Border Patrol officers increased by 500 percent,

---

37. Ron Nixon, "As Donald Trump Calls for Wall on Mexican Border, Smugglers Dig Tunnels," *New York Times*, September 1, 2016, *www.nytimes.com/2016/09/02/us /us-mexico-border-wall-tunnels.html?_r=0.*

38. Douglas S. Massey, and Karen A. Pren, "Unintended Consequences of US Immigration Policy: Explaining the Post-1965 Surge from Latin America," *Population and Development Review* 38.1 (2012): 1–29, *https://www.ncbi.nlm.nih.gov/pmc /articles/PMC3407978/.*

and the budget ballooned twentyfold. Hundreds of miles of walls were built. In the same period, the number of unauthorized persons grew from three million to twelve million. Despite these measures, the likelihood of a person eventually making it across the border never dipped below 95 percent. Proponents are considering spending additional billions on border barriers, despite the fact that the net flow of Mexicans has been at zero since 2008.[39]

Don Felipe

Don Felipe grew up in Santa Ana, Mexico. He spent most of his youth working in the fields with his father, spending only four years in school. He migrated to work in Mexico City to put another brother through school. After landing a series of better jobs, he opened a laundromat and became a key support of his extended family. To improve his lot further, he migrated to Atlanta where he worked in construction, eventually establishing a stonemason business. Atlanta boomed and Don Felipe thrived. He became the go-to person for several generations of young people from Santa Ana looking to find work in Atlanta. Although Don Felipe took advantage of the 1986 amnesty to become a U.S. citizen, many of the young people that he helped get a start remain locked in the shadow world of the unauthorized.[40]

The lack of a "line" to get into and the discussion of building a wall, in conjunction with the employment needs of U.S. employers not met by U.S. workers, has created a situation where millions of undocumented people are in the United States without permission.

---

39. Douglas Massey, Jorge Durand, and Karen A. Pren, "Why Border Enforcement Backfired," *American Journal of Sociology* 121, no. 5 (March 2016): 1557–1600. Ironically, the ones now practicing circular migration are those Mexican Americans who have legal status, while the unauthorized are locked in place. Massey and his coauthors argue that the most important variable that explains this zero net flow is the sharp decline in the Mexican fertility rate, from 7.2 children per woman in 1965 to 2.3 children in 2016.

40. Marie Friedmann Marquardt, Timothy J. Steigenga, Philip J. Williams, and Manual A. Vasquez, *Living Illegal: The Human Face of Unauthorized Immigration* (New York: New Press, 2011), 20–24, 29–30.

Employers are anticipating serious employee shortages because many of the workers who have worked for them for decades are getting old and can no longer do hard labor. As they leave the jobs, there are not enough workers to fill them. If visa availability reflected labor needs, then border enforcement officials could focus their attention on criminal elements that actually pose a danger, rather than monitoring migration flows of labor. While there are serious issues with drug smuggling and human trafficking, restrictionists are mistaken in claiming that migrants steal the jobs of U.S. citizens. Most of these migrants do not have the option of "getting in line," and they are unlikely to be stopped by a wall.

Reflect and Discuss

1. Which response to the restrictionist arguments do you find most persuasive? Which seem least persuasive? On what aspects of the debate do you feel the need to do more research in order to have a position?

2. Did any of the statistics presented in this chapter lead you to think about either legal or unauthorized immigration to the United States in a new way? Explain.

3. Look again at the stories of Alex Torrenegra and Don Felipe. What do they tell you about what is working and what is not working in current immigration policies?

Part 2

Judge—Thinking Through Complex Realities

Part 2 explores step two of the see-judge-act process. Once the work of seeing has opened one's eyes to the realities at hand, one makes judgments about these data: What are the problems, wrongs, and injustices that must be addressed? This section embodies the "judge" step, which makes use of principles drawn from the social teaching of the Catholic Church and applies them to aspects of global migration. The judgments formed here will then become the basis for determining actions aimed at ameliorating injustice—the third step in the see-judge-act process.

CHAPTER 5

Developing an Evaluative, Ethical Framework

One of the authors of this book, Liz Collier, joined the Jesuit Volunteer Corps (JVC) as a volunteer for a year after graduating from college. She wanted to utilize her Spanish degree and escape Midwestern winters, so she applied to JVC: South. She was offered a job in a pro bono legal aid office in Houston, Texas, working full-time with asylum applicants who had fled persecution in their home countries and managed to enter the United States. She encountered many victims of rape, torture, and death threats, and some whose families had been murdered right in front of them. Despite the involvement of dedicated lawyers, every case except one that year was denied by an immigration judge.[1] Liz tried to reconcile what was happening in the U.S. political and judicial system and the horrors that the asylum applicants had suffered with her Catholic faith. She knew much about the Church's teaching on such topics as abortion, euthanasia, sexual ethics, the sacraments, and the importance of a relationship with God. But she did not know what the Church had to say about the injustice she was seeing.

Toward the end of her year in JVC, a speaker introduced her to a body of the Catholic Church's teaching called Catholic social teaching (CST). This teaching was the missing link. It gave her a framework for reflecting on injustice and for discerning what her responsibility as a Christian might be. Her work with immigrants,

---

1. Chico Harlan, "In an Immigration Court that Nearly Always Says No, a Lawyer's Spirit Is Broken," *Washington Post*, Business, October 11, 2016, *www.washingtonpost .com/business/economy/in-an-immigration-court-that-nearly-always-says-no-a-lawyers -spirit-is-broken/2016/10/11/05f43a8e-8eee-11e6-a6a3-d50061aa9fae_story.html ?hpid=hp_hp-more-top-stories_immigrationlawyer-845am%3Ahomepage%2Fstory.*

and the revelation of CST, made her passionate about giving college students opportunities to work with vulnerable populations and to think through how to create a more just world. Her experience had enabled her to "see"; the resources of her faith and of CST enabled her to "judge." Together they laid the foundation for effective action.

Catholic Social Teaching

The Church has always pondered what it means for a person of faith to grapple with issues in the economic, political, and social spheres. Answers have developed and been conveyed in word and action through avenues such as homilies, pastoral letters, theological treatises, catechetical materials, religious orders, lay movements for justice, and nonprofit organizations working on behalf of the marginalized and vulnerable.

Beginning in 1891, an official body of written teaching was established with the promulgation of Pope Leo XIII's encyclical, *Rerum novarum* (*On the Condition of Labor*). The phrase *modern Catholic social teaching* refers to the official body of teaching that began with this document. In *Rerum novarum*, the Church reflected on the realities that workers faced during the Industrial Revolution. It gleaned principles and values from Scripture, tradition, and other sources of wisdom to aid workers, unions, managers, and owners in determining their moral responsibilities. Since then, Church leaders at the local, regional, and global levels have continued to write about and give guidance on important social, political, and economic issues. Catholic social teaching develops as new issues emerge and the Church explores them in light of Scripture, tradition, and findings from disciplines such as economics, psychology, and political theory.

Migration has been an integral experience and a recurring metaphor throughout Jewish and Christian tradition. While the themes of welcoming the stranger and Christian hospitality arose often in the Church's history in response to migration issues, it wasn't until 1952 that an apostolic constitution dedicated specifically to migration was promulgated, Pope Pius XII's *Exsul familia*. Since then the Church's teaching on migration has developed as people at many levels within the institutional Church have written, spoken, and organized on behalf of migrants.

CST offers many concepts and principles central to understanding and evaluating issues of justice within the social, economic, and political spheres. This book focuses on four concepts that form part of the theological foundation of CST: human dignity, the common good, stewardship, and the preferential option for the poor.[2]

Human Dignity

The Church affirms the God-given dignity of every person and calls individuals to see themselves and everyone they encounter in this light. The book of Genesis makes clear that everything created by God is, at its core, good—it has an intrinsic goodness. When the creation story reaches the point where God creates humans, we learn that people are created in the "image and likeness" of God and that, with the addition of humankind, God sees creation as "very good" (Gen. 1:26,31). Therefore, Christians believe that God has created *every* person, regardless of age, ability, race, religion, socioeconomic status, education level, gender, or any other trait, with God's own image and likeness at the center of his or her being. This makes every human precious to God and worthy of being treated as such. How people care for themselves and treat others either nurtures their own and others' dignity or diminishes it. A close look at biblical accounts of Jesus' interactions with those he encountered reveals a deep love and respect for those to whom he ministered. Jesus treated everyone with reverence commensurate with their dignity.

Human dignity is central to CST's understanding of what it means to be human. Quoting Saint Pope John Paul II's 1991 papal encyclical *Centesimus annus*, the U.S. Catholic bishops write, "Human persons are willed by God; they are imprinted with God's image. Their dignity does not come from the work they do, but from the persons they are."[3] *Gaudium et spes* (*Pastoral Constitution on the*

---

2. For a more comprehensive treatment of the concepts and principles of CST, see "Seven Themes of Catholic Social Teaching," United States Conference of Catholic Bishops, *www.usccb.org/beliefs-and-teachings/what-we-believe/catholic-social-teaching /seven-themes-of-catholic-social-teaching.cfm*.

3. "Life and Dignity of the Human Person," United States Conference of Catholic Bishops, *www.usccb.org/beliefs-and-teachings/what-we-believe/catholic-social-teaching /life-and-dignity-of-the-human-person.cfm*, quoting paragraph 11 of Saint Pope John Paul II's *Centesimus annus*.

Church in the Modern World, 1963), a Vatican II document, says, "This council lays stress on reverence for the human person; everyone must consider one's every neighbor without exception as another self, taking into account first of all life and the means necessary for living it with dignity, so as not to imitate the rich man who had no concern for the poor man Lazarus."[4]

Human dignity and the duty of each person and community to ensure that everyone's dignity is realized is at the heart of the Church's teaching on migration. In his 2014 Message on the World Day of Migrants and Refugees, Pope Francis stated,

> While it is true that migrations often reveal failures and shortcomings on the part of States and the international community, they also point to the aspiration of humanity to enjoy a unity marked by respect for differences, by attitudes of acceptance and hospitality which enable an equitable sharing of the world's goods, and by the protection and the advancement of the dignity and centrality of each human being.[5]

Pope Francis has made it his practice to greet refugees individually and hear their stories. After Pope Francis visited the U.S.-Mexican border, Cardinal Seán Patrick O'Malley observed, "[Pope Francis] always begins with the person, with his or her dignity, with their humanity, with their needs, and with the dangers they face each day. His ministry has consistently been about reaching across boundaries and frontiers, which seem impregnable, but in fact are open to human initiatives and humane policies."[6] O'Malley went on to say that while we may tend to categorize people on the move as migrants or refugees, Syrians, or Muslims, these categories do not capture the deepest truth of migration: "Before all else in every migrant, refugee, or family escaping danger and destitution we meet

4. "Dignity," Catholic Charities of St. Paul and Minneapolis, Minnesota, quoting paragraph 27 of Vatican Council II, *Gaudium et spes*, *www.cctwincities.org /education-advocacy/catholic-social-teaching/notable-quotations/dignity/*.

5. Pope Francis, "Migrants and Refugees: Towards a Better World," 2014, *https:// cliniclegal.org/sites/default/files/papal_messages_for_the_world_day_of_migrants_and _refugees.pdf*.

6. "Cardinal: US Immigration Policy Must Combine Compassion and Safety," *Crux*, February 18, 2016, *https://cruxnow.com/church/2016/02/18/cardinal-us -immigration-policy-must-combine-compassion-and-safety/*.

the human person, sharing our humanity, sharing our vulnerability to conditions of war, conflict, poverty, and discrimination."[7] It is this striving to look into the eyes of each immigrant and hear their stories that the pope believes moves the human heart to protect the sanctity of these lives. In response to President Trump's January 27, 2017, order "Protecting the Nation from Foreign Terrorist Entry into the United States," which, among other things, blocked Syrian refugees from entering the United States, CRS's president and CEO, Sean Callahan, explained that refugees already go through "extreme vetting" and "Christian faith calls on us to serve people based on need, not creed. We are called to welcome the Stranger. This is a time for the United States to be the Good Samaritan."[8]

The Common Good

Also central to the Church's understanding of what it means to be human is our social nature—we belong to each other. People live their lives in communities: families, neighborhoods, schools, places of employment, places of worship, cities, and nations. People meet their physical, social, spiritual, educational, and emotional needs within communities, which also play an integral role in who we become. These communities provide role models, value systems, and frames of reference, while also meeting people's basic needs. The systems that surround individuals and communities must provide goods, resources, opportunities, and conditions for people to flourish.

The human person's social nature underlies Catholic social teaching's principle of the common good.[9] *Gaudium et spes* defines the common good as "the sum of those conditions of social life which allow social groups and their individual members relatively thorough and ready access to their own fulfillment."[10] This means that

---

7. Ibid.

8. Press release, "CRS Calls for Refugee Ban to Be Suspended: More Humane Approach Needed," January 31, 2017, *www.crs.org/media-center/news-release/crs-calls-for-refugee-ban-to-be-suspended*.

9. See "The Principle of the Common Good: The 10 Second Summary," Center of Concern, University of Notre Dame, *www.coc.org/files/principle.pdf*.

10. Vatican Council II, *Gaudium et spes*, no. 26 (December 7, 1965), in *Catholic Social Thought: The Documentary Heritage*, ed. David J. O'Brien and Thomas A. Shannon (Orbis: New York, 1992), 181.

individuals, communities, political entities, and other organizations have a responsibility to work together to provide everyone with that which is necessary for human flourishing. According to CST, these necessities go beyond basic food, clothing, and shelter, to include education, healthcare, freedom to worship, and even leisure time. They cover the human person's physical, emotional, psychological, and spiritual needs. "The common good does not consist in the simple sum of the particular goods of each subject of a social entity. Belonging to everyone and to each person, it is and remains, common, . . . because only together is it possible to attain it, to increase it and safeguard its effectiveness."[11] CST charges each person with discerning how he or she can contribute to the common good, to meet the needs and foster the flourishing of others. Individuals consider what they have to give in light of the needs of others.

Stewardship

Every member of the human community has passions, resources, and abilities. If all people contribute to the community, they exercise and enhance their own dignity and build the common good. The book of Genesis presents humans as cocreators with God. Humans have a responsibility to care for God's creation; they also have a responsibility to use their gifts to cooperate with God's continuing work of creation. According to Saint Pope John Paul II, creation means both the natural world and that which people have developed using natural resources.

The participation of every person strengthens a community's pursuit of the common good. Needs go unmet when some are kept from participating and others view their talents, possessions, and resources as solely their own. All of creation is meant to serve the entire human community. While individuals may possess certain resources, according to Catholic social teaching these gifts are to be shared. In other words, all goods have a social destination. This means people are caretakers, or stewards, of their gifts, their talents, their resources, and the natural world. They are obligated to use their gifts in the service of their community. This does not mean that there

---

11. *Compendium of the Social Doctrine of the Catholic Church* (United States Conference of Catholic Bishops: Washington, DC, 2004), no. 164, *http://www.usccb.org /beliefs-and-teachings/what-we-believe/catechism/compendium/index.cfm.*

shouldn't be private property. Stewards consider how to serve others through the use of their gifts and possessions, which may include financial resources, a car, the ability to read, a job skill, or other resources. "God destined the earth and all it contains for all people and nations so that all created things would be shared fairly by all humankind under the guidance of justice, tempered by charity."[12]

When visiting migrants on the Italian island of Lampedusa, Pope Francis recounted the Spanish comedy where the townspeople of Fuente Ovejuna kill their tyrant governor in such a way that no one knows who is guilty. When the judge asks who killed the governor, he is simply told, "Fuente Ovejuna," meaning, everyone and no one. Pope Francis likened this to the way many people deal with the migrant crisis:

> The culture of comfort, which makes us think only of ourselves, makes us insensitive to the cries of other people, makes us live in soap bubbles which, however lovely, are

© REUTERS / Alamy Stock Photo

Pope Francis, as one of the earliest acts of his papacy, travelled to Lampedusa, Italy, where he greeted African migrants who had crossed the Saharan Desert and the Mediterranean Sea.

12. *Gaudium et spes*, no. 69.

insubstantial; they offer a fleeting and empty illusion which results in indifference to others; indeed, it even leads to the globalization of indifference. In this globalized world, we have fallen into globalized indifference. We have become used to the suffering of others: it doesn't affect me; it doesn't concern me; it's none of my business![13]

Being a steward requires one to act in ways commensurate with one's particular situation. This could mean choosing a career where one works with vulnerable populations, advocates for others, or serves the community in other ways. It might mean volunteering with a local organization or group, donating money or services, engaging in civil disobedience, or organizing people to tackle an issue together. This participation, or stewardship, enhances everyone's dignity and also the common good. Respecting human dignity, acting as a steward, and fostering the common good are all interconnected.

The Preferential Option for the Poor

Many people throughout the world suffer marginalization by systems, social structures, and civil and political leaders. These people are the subject of a fourth principle of CST: the preferential option for the poor.

This principle derives directly from Scripture. The Old Testament repeatedly instructs God's people to hear and respond to the cries of the poor, know their needs and attend to them, and forgive debts.[14] These Scriptures frequently single out the widow, the orphan, and the alien as particularly vulnerable people, unable to meet their own needs within the boundaries set by society, and therefore in particular need of help.[15] In Christian Scripture and tradition, Jesus' birth and early years comprise a story of being "on the move,"[16] including his family's flight from their homeland due to persecution

---

13. "Homily of Holy Father Francis: 'Arena' Sports Camp, Salina Quarter, 8 July 2013," *http://w2.vatican.va/content/francesco/en/homilies/2013/documents/papa-francesco_20130708_omelia-lampedusa.html.*

14. Examples include Deut. 15; Job 34:25–28; Ps. 34; Prov. 21:13; 22:22–23.

15. Examples include Exod. 22:21-25; Lev. 19:33; Deut. 10:18; Isa. 1:17; Jer. 22:3.

16. Luke 2:1–7.

by the political powers of that time.[17] Throughout the New Testament, Jesus interacts with those who are diminished by the social, religious, and political structures of his day, such as women, Samaritans, and tax collectors. In Matthew 25, Jesus tells his hearers that their salvation is dependent upon feeding the hungry, clothing the naked, visiting those in prison, and welcoming the stranger. To be Christian means giving preferential treatment to those whose human dignity is diminished. To be Christian also means welcoming and helping those whose communities are not flourishing. While all people are to be viewed as brothers and sisters because they are precious in God's eyes, those with the most pressing needs must be central to Christian stewardship.

Since the beginning of his papacy, Pope Francis has lived out the preferential option for the poor, particularly on migration issues. While continuing the many ministries already in place at the Vatican, he also asked seminaries, convents, and other groups in the Italian Church to house as many immigrants as they could. These groups coordinated with the Italian government and Caritas Internationalis to provide beds for seven thousand migrants.[18] Italian bishop Nunzio Galatino said that the Pope's "teaching is taking us back to the very core of the Christian message, which prevents, for those who want to accept it and live it, turning their backs on the needy."[19] Many faith-based organizations take this option for the poor as their *raison d'etre*. Catholic Relief Services is one such organization that embodies this preferential option in their self-understanding: "In every economic, political and social decision, a weighted concern must be given to the needs of the poorest and most vulnerable. When we do this we strengthen the entire community, because the powerlessness of any member wounds the rest of society."[20] Since most migrants leave their homes due to violence, poverty, lack of economic opportunity, the effects of climate change, and other dehumanizing conditions, their plight generally falls under this preferential option.

---

17. Matt. 2:16–23.

18. Ines San Martin, "Europe's Bishops Echo Pope Francis on the 'Human Tragedy' of Migrants," *Crux* (August 20, 2015), *https://cruxnow.com/church/2015/08/20/europes-bishops-echo-pope-francis-on-the-human-tragedy-of-migrants/*.

19. Ibid.

20. "Guiding Principles," Catholic Relief Services, *www.crs.org/about/guiding-principles*.

Applying CST to the Issue of Migration

Christians committed to justice use the concepts of human dignity, stewardship, common good, and preferential option for the poor, as well as others developed by the Catholic tradition,[21] as a lens to examine contemporary social issues, including immigration. A key document to emerge from such examination is "Strangers No Longer: Together on the Journey of Hope" (2003), written collaboratively by the bishops of the United States and Mexico.[22] In this document, the bishops demonstrate how the foundational concepts of CST can be a lens through which people see the plight of migrants and then act on their behalf. In developing the teaching on migration, the bishops gathered as much information as they could from people involved with migration—from Border Patrol agents to migrants, the faith communities that help migrants, and government officials. These are two characteristics of the process through which CST develops: (1) gathering sources of wisdom and insight from many disciplines and the lived experience of people involved in the issue at hand, in order to determine what enhances or diminishes dignity, community, justice, and the experience of the most marginalized, and (2) assessing the knowledge gained in light of Scripture and tradition. The history of hospitality to the stranger, the migrant experience of the Israelites and the Holy Family, along with the history of migration to the Americas and relationship of Christianity to the history of migration, inform how people view the complicated issues of migration.

The Church's teaching on migration has come to focus on five principles:[23]

1. People Have a Right to Find Opportunity in their Homeland. Central to one's human dignity is one's homeland. Language, religion, culture, and geography indelibly form who people are and give them

---

21. To learn about the broader set of principles that make up CST, see "Seven Themes of Catholic Social Teaching," *www.usccb.org/beliefs-and-teachings/what-we-believe/catholic-social-teaching/seven-themes-of-catholic-social-teaching.cfm.*

22. "Strangers No Longer: Together on the Journey of Hope," United States Conference of Catholic Bishops, *www.usccb.org/issues-and-action/human-life-and-dignity/immigration/strangers-no-longer-together-on-the-journey-of-hope.cfm.*

23. Ibid.

a "home." Most people want to live their lives in the land of their birth. The vast majority of people who migrate do so because they are not able to meet their basic needs in their homeland. Because one's birthplace is central to one's identity, the first priority is to work for resolution of the issues that cause people to migrate from their places of origin.

2. People Have a Right to Migrate to Support Themselves and Their Families. If remaining in one's own country is not feasible, then this second principle applies. People who are not able to find employment and opportunity in their homelands must be able to move to a location where they can meet these needs. This right to migrate means that there is a corresponding duty on the part of those who live in areas with opportunity to show hospitality.

3. Sovereign Nations Have the Right to Control Their Borders. The third principle respects the boundaries that nations have created in the political sphere. This right is not absolute, however: people cannot be refused entry solely to enable the receiving country to maintain a high standard of living. This duty relates most strongly to those countries that have opportunity available. This principle flows from the CST conviction that the human person precedes the state, which means that human dignity and human flourishing are ultimate realities that precede the current human-created political structures and rules. While those structures and rules should be respected, they are not more important than the right of human beings to support themselves and their families. The goods of the earth and all human-created resources are a gift from God to the entire human community. Countries that are on the receiving end of migration are required to be stewards of their accessible resources.

4. Refugees and Asylum Seekers Should Be Afforded Protection. This is a challenging principle today because of the more than sixty-five million people who have had to flee their homes. The pressure this migration places on countries in surrounding regions creates hardship for many, which requires the global community to work to resolve the problems prompting migration, house people during their transition, and find permanent homes for people outside of the refugee camps. The bishops are concerned about the incarceration rates faced by people who flee one country and enter another without permission. They are concerned also about asylum cases not being adjudicated in a fair and consistent manner. Many laws govern these cases, most of which are unknown to those who have fled persecution and violence. Lack of understanding of the receiving nations' complex immigration laws often results in people being deported back to countries where their lives are in danger.

Everyone deserves protection, particularly those in the most vulnerable positions in society. This is due to everyone's inherent dignity, as well as the Catholic understanding that diminishing anyone's dignity diminishes everyone's dignity. The jails and detention centers where migrants are often held are not environments conducive to fulfilling the needs of someone experiencing a crisis. Often even minimal basic human needs go unmet. Frequently government officials adjudicate cases inadequately or even unfairly, to the detriment of the common good. Because migrants often are the most vulnerable, they do not have economic power, political power, or connections of any kind in the receiving country. They are voiceless, in need of the voices and protection of people in the receiving communities.

5. The Human Dignity and Human Rights of Undocumented Migrants Should Be Respected. The centrality of the human dignity and human rights of "the other" need to frame any discussion of migration. When the "see" step is neglected, the humanity of the migrant disappears. When coupled with the myths about immigration, the rhetoric surrounding the plight of undocumented people can result in ill-conceived policy proposals and dehumanizing treatment of some of society's most vulnerable human beings.

Rights and Stewardship

Most of the Church's principles on migration include the term "right." If a person has a "right" to something, then there is another person or community that has a duty, or responsibility, to ensure that the right is realized. Impediments to the realization of rights are often the causes of migration. Stewardship begins when people ask themselves what they can contribute: What work can I perform that might serve others? What expertise do I have that can help at the micro- or macro-level of the issues faced by migrants? What resources do I have that might serve the most vulnerable in my community? The causes of migration require a wide range of expertise to tackle. Opportunities to work on behalf of others are many.

Reflect and Discuss

1. In what ways has your dignity been enhanced and developed by others? In what ways has it been diminished?

2. In what ways have you enhanced someone else's dignity? Have you ever diminished someone else's dignity?

3. Make a list of everything you believe must be part of the common good for everyone in the community truly to flourish.

4. Describe someone you know who is a steward of his or her talents, passions, or resources. How might you mirror this person in supporting the common good?

5. In what ways have you been or might you be a steward over your talents, passions, or resources?

6. As noted, the Scriptures claim that God hears the "cries of the poor." Who are these poor today? In what ways are people responding to these cries?

7. What about Catholic social teaching do you find most compelling? What needs further clarification?

Part 3

Act—Responding on Behalf of Refugees, Internally Displaced People, and Migrants

Part 1 explored some realities of global migration today, and part 2 introduced Catholic social teaching (CST), which provides ethical and theological principles for evaluating migration issues. Part 3, addressing step three in the see-judge-act process, explores individual and collective responses to unjust situations affecting migrants, one of the most pressing ethical issues of our time. Many of the courses of action that one might take involve participating in nongovernmental organizations (NGOs) that work with immigrants; some of these options are explored in chapter 6, with special attention to the work of Catholic Relief Services. Another important avenue for change involves working with local and national governments to achieve immigration reform; chapter 7 examines the problems with the current system in the United States, together with proposals for bringing the system more in line with CST. Finally, chapter 8 considers some of the factors that lead concerned individuals to get involved—to proceed from concern to action.

CHAPTER **6**

Collective Action: The Role of NGOs in International Development

The forces that make and remake our world are shifting. Many people think of international relations as dominated by nation-states pursuing their own interests. However, in the aftermath of World War II, new actors made their way onto the international stage: the United Nations and its numerous agencies, international economic organizations like the World Bank and the World Trade Organization, and multinational corporations. The adoption of the Universal Declaration on Human Rights in 1948 and its subsequent application to areas like the rights of refugees and migrants have fostered the rise of thousands of nongovernmental organizations (NGOs) that pressure nation-states to adhere to principles that foster and safeguard the dignity of all human beings. Increasingly networked with one another, these NGOs form what many are calling a "global civil society."

> [Global civil society is] an unfinished product that consists of sometimes thick, sometimes thin stretched networks . . . of socioeconomic institutions and actors who organize themselves across borders, with the deliberate aim of drawing the world together in new ways. These nongovernmental institutions and actors tend to pluralize power and to problematize violence; consequently their peaceful or "civil" effects are felt everywhere.[1]

---

1. John Keane, *Global Civil Society?* (Cambridge: University of Cambridge Press, 2003), 8. On global civil society as an independent force in international relations, see Charles R. Strain, *The Prophet and the Bodhisattva: Daniel Berrigan, Thich Nhat Hanh and the Ethics of Peace and Justice* (Eugene, OR: Wipf and Stock, 2014), 154–63, 193–201.

Catholic Relief Services (CRS), with its grounding in Catholic social teaching (CST), its connections to a universal Church, and its partner organizations in *Caritas Internationalis*, is positioned to make important contributions to the workings of the globalized context. In fact, CRS shares, with other faith-based organizations, distinctive approaches to meeting the needs of vulnerable peoples and human rights. Faith-based NGOs have important advantages:

- They are not constrained by legalistic definitions of who counts as a refugee or forced migrant.
- They are closely connected to local congregations and, therefore, have access to grassroots, culturally sensitive knowledge of the crisis situation, in contrast to aid agencies that "parachute" into the situation from elsewhere.
- They are present before, during, and after the crisis arises. Their local congregations are part of the community. They remain working with "forgotten" displaced peoples after the spotlight of international attention has shifted elsewhere.
- They are often seen as more legitimate than government officials, and thus are often more trusted.
- They are committed to a sustained spiritual life, which offers strong support to those in the midst of crisis.[2]

Integral Human Development

Faith-based organizations like CRS, however, need something more than general ethical principles and a close working relationship with local communities to guide collective action, something that bridges the gap between judgment and action or what some have called an "operational principle."[3] For CRS, the concept of "integral human

---

2. This last point is the most important. See James Thomson, "Local Faith Actors and Protection in Complex and Insecure Environments," *Forced Migration Review* 48 (November 2014): 5–6; Joe Hampson, Thomas M. Crea, Rocio Calvo, Francisco Alvarez, "The Value of Accompaniment," *Forced Migration Review* 48 (November 2014): 7–8; Robert Cruickshank and Cat Cowley, "Faith Motivation and Effectiveness: A Catholic Experience," *Forced Migration Review* 48 (November 2014): 18–19; see also this entire issue, "Faith and Responses to Displacement," at *www.fmreview.org/faith*.

3. Agbonkhiammeghe Orobator, "Ethical Issues in the Practices and Policies of Refugee Serving NGOs and Donors," in *Refugee Rights: Ethics, Advocacy and Africa*, ed. David Hollenbach, SJ (Washington, DC: Georgetown University Press, 2008), 238.

development" (IHD) provides that practical guidance. In response to requests from its field staff for guidance on how to implement CST in actual programs, CRS developed "A User's Guide to Integral Human Development."[4] Pope Paul VI first articulated this concept in CST in his encyclical *Populorum Progressio* (*On the Development of Peoples*, 1967). "Development cannot be limited to mere economic growth. In order to be authentic, it must be complete: integral, that is, it has to promote the good of every man and of the whole man."[5] The "User's Guide" spells out the meaning of IHD by analyzing it as both a goal and a process.

> As a goal for CRS, IHD suggests a state of personal well-being in the context of just and peaceful relationships and a thriving environment. It is the sustained growth that everyone has the right to enjoy and represents an individual's cultural, economic, political, social and spiritual wholeness. . . . IHD also refers to the process by which a person achieves this well-being and common good. . . . In practice, this means that CRS must develop a common understanding of IHD with our partners and then jointly take a holistic approach to development. . . . Our collaborative work must consider the different dimensions of the whole person and of society, including social and environmental sustainability. It means we must bridge the gap between emergencies and development; between the lives of the poor and unjust policies, systems and practices; and between individual well-being and the common good.[6]

We have seen numerous examples of how CRS seeks to "bridge the gap between emergencies and development": educating refugee children and creating strategies for healing their traumas, helping

---

4. Geoff Heinrich, David Leege, and Carrie Miller, "A User's Guide to Integral Human Development: Practical Guidance for CRS Staff and Partners," Catholic Relief Services, 2008, *www.crs.org/sites/default/files/tools-research/users-guide-to -integral-human-development.pdf.*

5. Pope Paul VI, *Populorum Progressio* (March 26, 1967), #14, *http://w2.vatican.va /content/paul-vi/en/encyclicals/documents/hf_p-vi_enc_26031967_populorum.html.* Translation from Heinrich et al., "A User's Guide to Integral Human Development," 2.

6. Heinrich et al., "A User's Guide to Integral Human Development," 2–3.

Syrian refugees in Egypt start small businesses, and assisting Ghanaian women in creating alternative sources of income when drought reduced agricultural productivity. CRS provides "market-based" emergency aid that helps local economies grow and absorb refugee populations while enhancing the autonomy of refugees. Helping communities become resilient is a way of avoiding forced displacement.

Pope Francis, in a speech to the United Nations, stated the clearest imperative governing IHD when he said, "To enable these real men and women to escape from extreme poverty, we must allow them to be the dignified agents of their own destiny. Integral human development and the full exercise of human dignity cannot be imposed."[7] CRS recommends using an IHD framework at every stage of the project development process, from strategic planning and project design to project evaluation. It is especially critical that Pope Francis' injunction be observed at the beginning of the process. "No one understands the context that the poor are living in," insists the User's Guide, "better than the poor themselves." (The nouns "refugees" or "migrants" could easily be substituted for the word "poor" in this sentence). A "Participatory Livelihoods Assessment" enables the community to express its felt needs, develop a common understanding of the issues, assess previous projects, enable the community to advocate for its own solutions with government officials and donors, and build the community in the process.[8]

As mentioned in chapter 2, CRS follows an asset-based community development strategy. CRS's process for promoting integral human development involves employing the following integrated strategies:[9]

- **assets:** help people identify resources they have access to
- **systems and structures:** help people identify the systems and structures that organize society
- **influence and access:** assist people in identifying who has the power needed to influence systems and structures

---

7. Pope Francis, "Address to the General Assembly of the United Nations" (September 25, 2015), *http://w2.vatican.va/content/francesco/en/speeches/2015/september /documents/papa-francesco_20150925_onu-visita.html.*

8. Heinrich et al., "A User's Guide to Integral Human Development," 17–18.

9. Ibid., 5.

- **risk and vulnerability:** help people identify threats and build resilience
- **strategies:** seek to understand how people can act to improve their lives and plan for the future
- **outcomes and feedback:** monitor and assess results and find ways to address people's needs that reinforce their capacities and their power to influence systems and structures

The elements of CRS's work to promote intergral human development are necessary for any project to succeed. Systems and structures constrain the actions of individuals and communities but once people analyze and understand them, they are better able to influence them. This book's treatment of refugees and migrants highlighted numerous examples of risks and vulnerabilities—from climate change and civil wars to the impact of treaties like NAFTA—that force people to move. If people are able to identify threats they are better able to build resilience. CRS aims to help people harness assets and work with and against those who hold power, building resilience to overcome shocks and systemic constraints. Making progress toward integral human development involves assessing whether an initiative helps people lead fuller and more productive lives and how it reinforces people's abilities and power for influence.[10]

Creating Communities of Entrepreneurs

CRS has joined the "microfinance revolution" as one key strategy for empowering poor people and poor communities.[11] On a study trip to the U.S.-Mexican border, students from DePaul University crowded into the cramped office of Bancomun in the city center of Nogales, Sonora, just minutes away from the border. They had been visiting with migrants and human rights organizations, staying with poor people living in the *colonias* perched on Nogales's many hills. The group had learned on the one hand that workers in the assembly factories (*maquilas*) along the border were unable to support their

---

10. Ibid., 5–8.

11. On this movement, see Muhammad Yunis, *Creating a World without Poverty* (New York: Public Affairs, 2007*)*.

families without someone sending remittances from "the other side." Crossing the Arizona desert, however, was very dangerous. Now, at Bancomun, they saw a ray of hope. "Many people are aware that Catholic social teaching emphasizes the right to migrate, but the tradition also upholds the right to remain in one's native

African women work together to collect deposits and grant loans to members of the CRS-sponsored Savings and Internal Lending Communities (SILC) program.

place. CRS-Mexico nurtures stories of hope within Mexico by developing human and financial assets among Mexicans so they can exercise that right to stay and find opportunity in their homeland."[12]

Bancomun is part of a global "microfinance" movement that provides loans at modest interest to poor people. Ordinary banks will not lend to poor people who lack collateral. Loan sharks will—but at exorbitant interest. Microfinance offers an alternative. Small groups gather savings and individual members take out small loans ($25–75). The group guarantees repayment of the loan and group members help each other stay on track with business plans.[13]

After a short lesson on microfinance, the students visited a woman whose microloan enabled her to buy equipment to produce tortillas in bulk and sell them to her neighbors. Such stories abound. One woman set up a seamstress shop. Another sells pastries, while a third sells party supplies. "When I worked as a *maquila* organizer, I realized how little the workers made," comments Yvonne Pazos, one of the organizers of Bancomun. "The people I'm working with in the bank have so much hope and want to take so much initiative. . . . It changes their lives. They realize that they don't have to be dependent on a *maquila* salary."[14] They also have found this hope without leaving home.

12. Jeffrey Odell Korgen, *Solidarity Will Transform the World: Stories of Hope from Catholic Relief Services* (Maryknoll, NY: Orbis, 2007), 13.

13. Ibid., 11–21. See also chapter 3. Bancomun claims a repayment rate of 95 percent.

14. Korgen, *Solidarity*, 19. Of course, one should not ignore the issue of justice here. *Maquilas* producing goods to be sold cheaply in America do not pay a living wage.

CRS discovered that even microloans can be challenging for poor people to repay, so it devised the SILC (savings and internal lending communities) program. Here the capital comes from the group's own savings. Trained private services providers take fledgling groups through the steps of setting up a group, handling savings, and deciding to whom to lend money. Over 88,000 SILC groups have saved more than $19 million and benefitted almost two million people.[15]

New Approaches to Aiding Refugees

To be sure, these development-focused programs are long-term strategies. Meanwhile, 65.3 million people are in limbo and current humanitarian aid practices can no longer cope with this burden of displaced human beings. In this context, *advocacy* becomes an important form of action alongside emergency aid and longer-term development projects, such as microfinance. In advance of a UN summit held in September 2016, CRS developed a set of recommendations for altering the ways in which humanitarian work is carried out. CRS called upon both the U.S. government and the international community to invest in these new ways of addressing the refugee crisis, including the following:

- Respond to the needs of vulnerable people whether or not they fit the legal definition of refugees.
- Given the predominance of protracted displacement, invest in longer-term projects (3–5 years).
- Build positive relations between host and hosted communities. Relieve the burden on the shoulders of developing countries, which host 86 percent of refugees.
- Invest in "noncamp" solutions that integrate refugees and internally displaced persons in surrounding communities.
- Prioritize projects that link emergency aid with longer-term development strategies.

---

15. "A World of Difference: An Interview with the President of CRS," *U.S. Catholic*, April 15, 2013, *www.uscatholic.org/articles/201304/world-difference-27161*; "About Savings-Led Microfinance," Catholic Relief Services, *www.crs.org/our-work -overseas/program-areas/savings-led-microfinance*; "Lives & Livelihoods: How Savings Groups Transform Lives," Catholic Relief Services, *www.crs.org/our-work-overseas /program-areas/microfinance/silc-road/impact*.

- Shift to market-based assistance (cash, vouchers, prepaid debit cards) wherever possible to boost local economies, create jobs, and support the agency of refugees.
- Train and work through local community organizations.
- Above all, push for political solutions to conflicts.[16]

Advocacy

CRS also advocates for particularly vulnerable groups of refugees and migrants. In summer 2014, the United States saw a huge influx of unaccompanied children from Central America seeking asylum. Rick Jones, CRS deputy regional director of Latin America and the Caribbean, testified before a Senate Homeland Security committee: "We are witnessing an exodus due to violence . . . in Central America," Jones said. Honduras, Guatemala, El Salvador, and Belize have four out of the five highest homicide rates in the world. Gangs employ "join-or-die" tactics and have even taken over hundreds of schools. "Increasing desperation has led many families, youth, and children to the inevitable conclusion that they have no choice but to flee. They are primarily fleeing violence, not poverty. They aren't just coming to the United States; in fact, other Central American countries have experienced a 712 percent increase in asylum claims between 2008–2013."[17] Jones called upon the State Department to implement "an orderly departure program for children and families who are in danger and meet the requirements for refugee protection." He pointed to the success of CRS's YouthBuild program in El Salvador, which has given six thousand out-of-school, unemployed, at-risk teenagers job-skills training and has placed them in jobs in more than 250 businesses.[18]

---

16. "Meeting the Challenges of the World's Refugee Crisis: CRS' Recommendations for a Path Forward," Catholic Relief Services, 2016, 8–12, www.crs.org /get-involved/advocate/public-policy/meeting-challenges-worlds-refugee-crisis-policy-brief.

17. Richard Jones, "Testimony. Hearing on Challenges at the Border: Examining and Addressing the Root Causes behind the Rise in Apprehensions at the Southern Border," July 16, 2014, 2, 4, www.hsgac.senate.gov/download/?id =5cc5b457-ce91-4420-902b-580c2002d136.

18. Ibid., 7, 11. Implicitly, Jones suggests that these Central American children meet the legal standard for claiming asylum. The core principle of the Convention on the Status of Refugees is that the host country may not force refugees to return to the country whose violence they have escaped.

CRS executive leadership met with legislators and government officials to urge the government not only to respond in a humanitarian way but also to address root causes by investing in the region.[19] CRS monitored the cases of these Central American children. In January 2016, it denounced a Homeland Security decision to round up and deport some of these children, a decision that involved even taking them from their families. CRS criticized Immigration and Customs Enforcement for putting these children in "grave danger" of violence from the gangs they fled. In July 2016, CRS applauded a new initiative by the Obama administration in which Costa Rica could be a safe haven for these children and their families while their cases went forward. CRS, however, made it clear that the United States was in no position to call upon other nations to address the needs of refuges if it did not develop a comprehensive system of refugee protection within its own region.[20]

Beyond Advocacy to Resistance: The Sanctuary Movement

While CRS's mission directs it to work with migrants and refugees overseas and to advocate for them within the United States, some Christians and members of other religious traditions feel called by their faith to take drastic action. Such was the case with the Sanctuary Movement of the 1980s. In the 1980s, civil wars broke out in several Central American countries. The U.S. government actively supported right-wing governments through military aid, training, and other resources. In those countries, people who advocated for justice and peace, including journalists, trade unionists, religious leaders, and others, were "disappeared" under the guise of preventing a communist takeover. In 1981, a death squad assassinated Oscar

19. The U.S. Congress has responded by investing $750 million in the region in FY 16.

20. "CRS Calls on the Obama Administration to Protect Children Fleeing Central America," Catholic Relief Services, January 6, 2016, *www.crs.org/media-center/news -release/crs-calls-on-obama-administration-protect-children-fleeing-central-america*; "CRS Applauds the Expansion of the Central American Refugee Resettlement Program," Catholic Relief Services, July 28, 2016, *www.crs.org/media-center/news-release /crs-applauds-expansion-central-american-refugee-resettlement-program*.

Romero, archbishop of San Salvador, as he was celebrating Mass. Salvadorans and Guatemalans who were fleeing for their lives often sought asylum in the United States, but their cases were routinely denied in the 1980s.

Responding to this crisis, Jim Corbett, an Arizona Quaker rancher, began aiding Central American asylum seekers in crossing the border. He enlisted the support of the Reverend John Fife, a Presbyterian minister in Tucson, whose church became a "sanctuary."[21]

In March 1982, the Sanctuary Movement leaders declared:

> We believe that justice and mercy require that people of conscience and faith actively assert our God-given right to aid anyone fleeing from persecution and murder. The current administration of the United States law prohibits us from sheltering these refugees from Central America. Therefore, we believe that administration of the law is immoral as well as illegal. . . . Until [deportation proceedings of refugees are stopped], we will not cease to extend the sanctuary of the church to undocumented people from Central America.[22]

Soon 237 churches and synagogues joined the movement, creating an "underground railroad" for refugees to find asylum in Canada. In 1985, Corbett, Fife, and other leaders of the movement were indicted, tried, and convicted but were sentenced to only probation. They returned to their work in rescuing endangered lives.[23]

Beginning in 2014, with new streams of refugees fleeing violence in Central America, some churches have recommitted themselves to offering sanctuary.

In a letter to President Obama, leaders of the movement declared, "We believe that the Sanctuary Movement today reveals

---

21. In medieval English law, a fugitive charged with a crime or someone persecuted in time of war could find refuge—i.e., sanctuary—in a church, safe from the coercive power of the rulers.

22. Gary MacEoin, ed., *Sanctuary* (San Francisco: Harper and Row, 1985), 19.

23. For a history of the Sanctuary Movement, see Rev. John Fife, "From the Sanctuary Movement to No More Deaths," in *Religious and Ethical Perspectives on Global Migration*, ed. Elizabeth W. Collier and Charles R. Strain (Lanham, MD: Lexington, 2014), 257–71.

Working with local churches and community organizations, CRS emergency teams are able to respond rapidly to crises in more than 100 countries.

the human cost and moral crisis caused by mass deportations, as well as the recent targeting of Central American families seeking asylum. We call on all people of faith and conscience to share our commitment to accompany immigrants facing racial profiling, workplace discrimination, raids, detention and deportation."[24]

Looking to the Future

The treatment of refugees by the United States and globally will not be fixed overnight. CRS and its collaborators work toward the goal of a transformed process in which migrants are treated with the care and dignity that is their right, as the principles of IHD require. The problems such NGOs face are complex. "Even more than their desire for a roof over their heads or a permanent home," CRS reports, "[Syrian and Iraqi refugees] profoundly wish that their children—many

---

24. "Sanctuary Movement," *www.sanctuary2014.org/*. See also Puck Lo, "Inside the New Sanctuary Movement That's Protecting Immigrants from ICE," *The Nation* (May 6, 2015), *https://www.thenation.com/article/inside-new-sanctuary-movement-thats -protecting-immigrants-ice/*. In the aftermath of the November 2016 election, groups ranging from the three largest U.S. cities to universities and religious communities have declared themselves as sanctuaries, but what is meant by the term is not always clear.

of whom have been severely traumatized—can return to school."[25] What seems like a straightforward task of getting Syrian children in Jordan or Turkey back to school turns out to be hugely difficult when government schools are overflowing with both native and refugee children. CRS has provided financial support for school uniforms and fees. Where it is needed, CRS has rented space, trained teachers, and provided school supplies. It offers "catch-up" classes for students who have been out of school for some time and has established parent-teacher associations. Many children who have witnessed the horrors of war have special needs. The signs of trauma among such children range from stuttering and panicking at loud sounds, to fears that someone is coming to get their parents. Keeping a refugee child alive is a challenge. Enabling that child to create a life worth living is the ultimate challenge for integral human development.

Reflect and Discuss

1. Examine the concept of integral human development (IHD). What is your own list of factors that must be met if each human being is to flourish?

2. What do you see as the strengths of CRS's recommendations for changing how aid is delivered to displaced individuals and communities? What might be some of the gaps or weaknesses of these recommendations?

3. What issues does the concept of sanctuary—a place that is immune to the removal power of law enforcement officials raise for you? Should there be such a sacred space? What issues do the two phases of the movement raise for you? What changes have occurred regarding the meaning and application of the concept of "sanctuary"?

4. What possibilities do you see on your campus or in your community for advocating for refugees and internally displaced people?

---

25. "Middle East Refugees Seek Education for their Children," Catholic Relief Services, *www.crs.org/stories/middle-east-refugees-seek-education-their-children.*

CHAPTER 7

U.S. Immigration Policy: Steps toward Reform

Chapter 5 looked at ethical concepts rooted in Catholic social teaching (CST). Chapter 6 considered how nongovernmental organizations are able to apply CST in working toward integral human development, with special attention to Catholic Relief Services programs overseas, where immigration issues are most pressing. This chapter considers the obligations of governments toward immigrants, with a focus on the problems of immigrants in the United States. The moral obligation to work toward the creation of the common good in one's communities, including one's nation, flows from CST's conception of human beings as "persons-in-community," not isolated individuals pursuing narrow self-interests.

People who agree with the ethical principles of CST may not be moved to action that promotes justice unless they have confronted their fears about immigrants. Fear is a powerful motivator and a number of politicians and pundits have tried their best to inflame the U.S. electorate's fears of unauthorized migrants. The first objective of Border Patrol's 2012–2016 strategic plan is to prevent terrorists from entering the United States; the plan refers to those who enter unauthorized as "dangerous."[1] Creating guilt by association is one way of

---

1. "2012–2016 Border Patrol Strategic Plan," U.S. Customs and Border Protection, *www.cbp.gov/sites/default/files/documents/bp_strategic_plan.pdf*. On the ways public discourse affects popular attitudes toward unauthorized migrants, see Charles R. Strain, "The Migrant, My Mother," in *Religious and Ethical Perspectives on Global Migration*, ed. Elizabeth W. Collier and Charles R. Strain (Lanham, MD: Lexington, 2014), 199–202, 205nn65–68.

enflaming fears and discouraging people who might be inspired to work for immigration reform.

Another pernicious form of public discourse has been the association of unauthorized migrants with increased criminal activity. This myth has been repeatedly proven false for more than a decade. The most recent report states categorically, "For every ethnic group without exception, incarceration rates among young men are lowest for immigrants. This holds true for the Mexicans, Salvadorans, and Guatemalans who make up the bulk of the undocumented population."[2] And yet the myth persists. One reason is that some politicians and media personalities perpetuate the myth, which can instill fear. Education about immigrants and immigration enables people to correct this misconception.

Rituals of Solidarity

Many who engage in ethical reflection on migration are prompted by personal experience; for example, one might meet an immigrant by chance, confront questionable information about migration issues, or learn about migration-related injustice through a course project. A person's movement from reflection to action then is sometimes enhanced by experiences of solidarity with those who are forced to leave their homes.

The ways in which people are interconnected are not always immediately apparent. The "Case of Corn," discussed in chapter 3, demonstrated how international treaties like NAFTA promoted by the U.S. government negatively affect subsistence farmers in Chiapas. The "Case of Coffee," in chapter 2, demonstrated how reliance on fossil fuels in the United States negatively affects coffee growers in Guatemala.

---

2. As cited in Jason L. Riley, "The Mythical Connection between Immigrants and Crime," *The Wall Street Journal*, July 14, 2015, *www.wsj.com/articles/the-mythical-connection-between-immigrants-and-crime-1436916798*. See Walter Ewig, Daniel E. Martinez, and Ruben Rumbaut, "The Criminalization of Immigration in the United States," American Immigration Council, July 13, 2015, *www.american immigrationcouncil.org/research/criminalization-immigration-united-states*. For earlier studies and the impact of falsehoods on public discourse, see Charles R. Strain, "No More Deaths," in *Religious and Ethical Perspectives on Global Migration*, ed. Collier and Strain, 293n52.

Religious rituals and practices can help forge the bonds of solidarity.[3] Two examples help illustrate. Italian theologian Gioacchino Campese suggests that the migrant path crossing into the United States is a "way of the cross."[4] Central American migrants face robbery and rape from gangs along the southern Mexican border, predatory "coyotes" on the northern border, and the brutal heat of the Sonoran desert—the Devil's Highway. Every Tuesday for more than a decade, Presbyterian minister Mark Adams has led a pilgrimage to the border that separates Douglas, Arizona, from Agua Prieta, Sonora, Mexico. On one such pilgrimage, DePaul University students and faculty carried bundles of white crosses with names printed on them—names of migrants who had died in the desert. Marching toward the border, they paused to read aloud the names and prop the crosses on the curb. As each name was read, the group chanted "*presente.*" The dead migrant was present, held in the pilgrims' hearts and prayers. Sadly, most of the crosses bore the inscription "*No identificato*" (no identification) in place of a name. Reaching the border, the

A woman from Agua Prieta, Sonora, Mexico, a member of "Healing Our Borders," looks toward the U.S.-Mexico border as she carries a cross with the name of an undocumented immigrant who died in the desert near Douglas, AZ.

© Hayne Palmour IV/San Diego Union-Tribune via ZUMA Wire

marchers stopped to reflect on the United States' inability to intelligently and credibly address the need for comprehensive immigration reform, instead focusing solely on beefing up border security in high-traffic areas, thereby channeling these migrants to their deaths.

---

3. The scriptures regularly encourage a sense of solidarity with the migrant. For example, in Leviticus 19:33–34 the Israelites are enjoined to care for the resident alien because they, too, had been aliens.

4. Gioacchino Campese, "¿Cuantos Mas? The Crucified Peoples at the U.S.-Mexico Border," in *A Promised Land, A Perilous Journey*, ed. Daniel G. Groody and Gioacchino Campese (Notre Dame, IN: University of Notre Dame Press, 2008): 271–98.

A second example is a ritual that has been performed at numerous locations along the southern border of the United States that modifies the traditional Mexican celebration of *Posada*. The Posada ritual reenacts Gospel accounts of the travail of Joseph and his pregnant wife, Mary, searching for shelter, hoping for basic hospitality. Now, Mexicans on one side of the border and Americans on the other side come together to celebrate *Posada*. In

San Diego bishop Robert McElroy leads a congregation on both sides of the U.S.-Mexico border celebrating a prayerful *Posada*.

some places, they can join hands and share Communion through the spaces in the metal fencing. In other places, this is forbidden. The participants remember immigrants who came to the United States looking for a new life. The wall, a barrier both physical and symbolic, separates people whose lives are deeply connected. At a deep level, however, the *Posada* ritual breaks through this barrier. "Every time we come together," one participant affirms, "the wall comes down slightly, and I believe that one day, it will come down completely."[5]

Strategies for Immigration Reform

One who has worked through the "see" and "judge" steps of the see-judge-act process and is motivated to act in response to immigration-related injustice must wrestle with specific recommendations. In the

5. Pierrette Hondagneu-Sotelo, *God's Heart Has No Borders* (Berkeley: University of California Press, 2008), 133–35, 191–92; "Advocates for Migration in Arizona and Sonora Gather for '*Posada*,'" *The Catholic Sun*, December 22, 2015, *www.catholicsun .org/2015/12/22/advocates-for-migrants-in-arizona-sonora-gather-at-border-for-posada/*. Father Daniel Groody speaks of his experience celebrating the Eucharist with a community on both sides of the border wall: "Unable to touch my Mexican neighbor except through some small holes in the fence, I became painfully aware of the unity we celebrated but the divisions that we experienced . . . for no other reason than we were born on different sides of the fence." Daniel Groody, "Fruit of the Vine and Work of Human Hands: Immigration and the Eucharist," *Worship* 80 no. 5 (September 2006): 386–87, *http://kellogg .nd.edu/faculty/fellows/dgroody/articles/Groody%20Article%20Fruit%20Vine.pdf*.

United States, all sides acknowledge that immigration laws are badly in need of reform. Yet Congress has been gridlocked on this issue for years.[6] The U.S. Conference of Catholic Bishops (USCCB) supports comprehensive immigration reform and opposes enforcement-only policies. In 2013, the USCCB articulated a set of six reform recommendations, consistent with CST, to guide ethical reflection and inform citizens' obligations.[7] In 2015, they articulated a seventh recommendation.[8] Many other organizations have developed recommendations as well. Religious organizations that have offered recommendations or general principles include the National Council of Churches, the Evangelical Immigration Table within the National Association of Evangelicals, and the American Friends Service Committee, a Quaker organization. Secular organizations that have developed recommendations include Amnesty International USA and the American Immigration Lawyers Association. Here are the seven recommendations of the USCCB and selected points of comparison with those of the other five organizations:[9]

---

6. In June 2013, the Senate passed a bipartisan reform bill that included some of the specific recommendations discussed here. The House of Representatives refused to consider the Senate's compromise bill. Seung Min Kim, "Senate Passes Immigration bill," *Politico*, June 28, 2013, *www.politico.com/story/2013/06/immigration-bill-2013-senate-passes-093530.*

7. "Catholic Church's Position on Immigration Reform," United States Conference of Catholic Bishops, Office of Migration Policy and Public Affairs, 2013, *www.usccb.org/issues-and-action/human-life-and-dignity/immigration/churchteachingon immigrationreform.cfm.*

8. "Unlocking Human Dignity: A Plan to Transform the U.S. Immigrant Detention System," United States Conference of Catholic Bishops, Center for Migration Studies, 2015, *www.usccb.org/about/migration-and-refugee-services/upload/unlocking-human -dignity.pdf.*

9. For more information, see "Resolution on Immigration and Call for Action," National Council of Churches, September 22, 2008, *www.nationalcouncilofchurches.us /common-witness/2008/immigration.php;* "A New Path: Toward a Humane Immigration Policy," American Friends Service Committee, February 2009, *www.afsc.org /sites/afsc.civicactions.net/files/documents/%20New%20Path%20full%20version%20.pdf;* "Evangelical Statement of Principles for Immigration Reform," Evangelical Immigration Table, *www.evangelicalimmigrationtable.com/sign-the-principles/;* "Amnesty International USA Voices Serious Concerns about Federal Immigration Proposal Priorities," Amnesty International USA, April 2010, *www.amnestyusa.org/news /press-releases/usa-amnesty-international-usa-voices-serious-concerns-about-federal -immigration-proposal-priorities;* and "Solutions that Work: A Policy Manual for Immigration Reform," American Immigration Lawyers Association, March 2010, *www.aila.org/infonet/policy-manual-for-immigration-reform.*

Earned Legalization. Each organization agreed that unauthorized immigrants living in the United States should have a path to legal permanent residence and, eventually, to citizenship. Unauthorized immigrants would need to pass security screening, pay fines or back taxes, have a good work history, and have no serious criminal record.

Future Worker Program. The U.S. Catholic bishops argued for reducing unauthorized migration by permitting migrants to enter the country legally for temporary work, with appropriate protection for basic rights, including a living wage. The National Council of Churches, Amnesty International USA, and the American Immigration Lawyers Association agreed. The Evangelical Immigration Table did not touch the issue and the American Friends Service Committee argued that previous guest workers' programs, like the *Bracero* program, and the current temporary worker visas are so exploitative that we should not repeat their failures. Instead, if workers in certain industries are needed, they should be provided with permanent residence status.

Family-Based Immigration Reform. This reform would increase the number of visas for family reunification and would streamline bureaucratic procedures to significantly reduce the excessive wait time. It would also end deportations that break apart families with members who are U.S. citizens and legal permanent residents. The six organizations agreed that these reforms are top priority, stressing that the family is the basic unit of society and central to its health.

Restoration of Due Process Rights. Because unauthorized migration is a civil offense, not a criminal offense,[10] U.S. law does not require the meeting of due process guarantees, which are mandated in criminal proceedings. Such due process requirements include, for example, the requirement that unaccompanied minors must be represented by an attorney in immigration court. Immigrant advocates argue that such civil rights are inalienable and should not depend upon citizenship. All the organizations except Evangelical Immigration Table called

---

10. An example of a civil offense would be parking a car in front of a fire hydrant. This offense may lead to a fine, but it is not an infraction that leads to imprisonment or a criminal record.

for this action. The Evangelical Immigration Table's commitment to "the rule of law," however, seems to include due process guarantees for anyone detained by Immigration and Customs Enforcement.

Addressing Root Causes.[11] The U.S. Catholic bishops insist that the global injustice underlying much of global migration be addressed by governments. The National Council of Churches and the American Friends Service Committee also strongly support this position. The American Friends Service Committee supports the right not to migrate, as have the bishops in other writings.

Enforcement. The U.S. Catholic bishops believe that the U.S. government's interception of unauthorized migrants who attempt to enter the United States is legitimate. They also believe that expanding opportunities for the legal entry of migrants will allow law enforcement to target the criminal activity of drug and human traffickers and would-be terrorists. Additionally, they call for honoring the rights of detained, unauthorized migrants. The National Council of Churches and the American Friends Service Committee emphasize that this combination of expanded legal opportunities and targeted law enforcement should include a demilitarization of the United States' southern border. The Evangelical Immigration Table argues that the borders must be secured and the rule of law enforced.[12]

Immigrant Detention System. The U.S. Catholic bishops have argued for a significant transformation of the current immigrant and refugee detention system. "Detention should not be used to deter illegal immigration or refugee-like flows, or as a means to evade U.S. sovereign responsibilities to protect those who have fled persecution. Its use should turn exclusively on an individualized determination of flight risk and danger."[13] Amnesty International USA, the American Friends Service Committee, and the American Immigration Lawyers Association agree and particularly condemn the housing of detainees

---

11. The bishops do not elaborate on what they see as root causes here. See, however, the earlier analysis of the impact of NAFTA in chapter 3, "The Case of Corn."

12. EIT does not explain the use of the term "rule of law." In the Catholic view, Christians are called to obey only just laws, not unjust laws. The rule of law is not an absolute injunction.

13. "Unlocking Human Dignity," United States Conference of Catholic Bishops.

in local jails and private prisons. Amnesty points out that asylum seekers who eventually were granted asylum averaged ten months of detention, which appears to be a clear violation of the U.N. Convention on the Status of Refugees. Only in rare cases of a threat to public safety should anyone be detained. Periodic check-in with designated community organizations, the American Friends Service Committee agrees, should replace a system of *de facto* incarceration without due process. Finally, the National Council of Churches calls for the significant expansion of the U.S. refugee and asylum program as reflecting the biblical command to show hospitality to the stranger.

Border Enforcement

Congress has failed to pass comprehensive immigration reform since 1986, but since then has spent hundreds of billions of dollars on control of the southern border. These funds have not treated the root causes of migration. More than a decade ago, human rights organizations, law enforcement chiefs, and local mayors from the borderlands formed a coalition of three border networks (Border Network for Human Rights, Border Action Network, and U.S.-Mexico Border and Immigration Task Force) to voice local concerns about border enforcement. Their recommendations, which still await enactment, are as follows:

Accountability. The coalition called for an end to racial profiling and an independent review of human rights violations by Border Patrol officers. The coalition pointed to studies in Texas and New Mexico that indicated that citizens made 40 percent of complaints about Border Patrol's human rights' violations. A decade later, a special integrity panel, convened by the secretary of the Department of Homeland Security, criticized Customs and Border Protection for its lack of transparency, inadequate internal investigations unit, unnecessary use of deadly force by Border Patrol officers, and "broken disciplinary process."[14]

---

14. "Final Report of the CBP Integrity Advisory Panel," March 15, 2016, Department of Homeland Security, *www.dhs.gov/sites/default/files/publications/HSAC%20 CBP%20IAP_Final%20Report_FINAL%20(accessible)_0.pdf.*

Border Walls. Current projects, the coalition argued, are expensive and unsuccessful. Moreover, "as a fundamental principle, public policies that address civilian social issues should not kill people."[15]

Local Law Enforcement. Well before groups like Amnesty International USA joined a chorus of critics, border leaders called for an end to deputizing local law enforcement officers to detain individuals not engaged in felony criminal activity for possible deportation by Immigration and Customs Enforcement. Such programs alienate immigrant communities from the police who are sworn to protect them.[16]

Examination of the recommendations summarized in this chapter may help one determine specific actions to address migration-related injustice.

Reflect and Discuss

1. What do you see as your moral obligation as a citizen to influence your nation's immigration policies?

2. View the video "San Diego, Tijuana Residents Have Cross-Border Christmas Celebration," KPBS, *www.kpbs.org /news/2015/dec/21/san-diego-and-tijuana-residents-have-cross -border-/* (time: 0:02:00). What role do such rituals play in leading people to act? In what ways do you develop a sense of solidarity with migrants in unjust circumstances?

3. Examine the recommendations for the reform of U.S. immigration policies and procedures advocated by the USCCB and the

---

15. "U.S.-Mexico Border Policy Report," Border Network for Human Rights, Border Action Network, and U.S.-Mexico Border and Immigration Task Force, November 2008, *https://law.utexas.edu/humanrights/borderwall/communities/municipalities-US -Mexico-Border-Policy-Report.pdf.*

16. Ibid. Congress under the 2008 "Secure Communities" program deputized police in participating communities to send fingerprints of even those who committed minor traffic offenses through Immigration and Customs Enforcement's databank. Casting a wide net for deportations, this act has led to racial profiling among law enforcement and fear and alienation in immigrant communities. See Marie Friedmann Marquardt, Timothy Steigenga, Philip Williams, and Manuel Vazquez, *Living Illegal: The Human Face of Unauthorized Immigration* (New York: New Press, 2011), 99–100, 139–54.

other five organizations mentioned in this chapter.[17] Do they treat adequately the issues raised, especially in chapters 3 and 4? Are they appropriate applications of CST? Why or why not? Which of these recommendations do you agree with? Disagree with? What ethical principles inform your judgments?

4. Identify a religious or secular organization not mentioned in this chapter that addresses immigration issues. What are its reform recommendations? Compare and contrast them with the six organizations mentioned in this chapter.

5. Develop your own list of immigration reforms. What might you do to see them enacted into law? With which groups might you work and share your reform proposals? What groups might you want to convince to adopt your proposals? How would you persuade them?

---

17. See footnote 9 for information about resources outlining these positions.

CHAPTER 8

Individual Action—Where Do We Go from Here?

Previous chapters have presented stories of refugees, internally displaced people, climate refugees, and authorized and unauthorized
migrants. This chapter begins with stories of those who decided to
act on behalf of those suffering to address some of the injustices that
they face.

Morgan Gruenewald was a political science and economics
major at Villanova when she interned with Catholic Relief Services
(CRS), developing and testing eLearning courses for CRS staff. After
spending a semester working with Save the Children in Uganda, she
returned to Villanova to become president of its CRS Ambassadors
program. Gruenewald followed up with a summer internship in
Madagascar working on a CRS water sanitation project.[1]

Eric Wise received his bachelor's degree from Oklahoma State
University and a master's in comparative politics from the American University in Cairo. He became a CRS international development fellow, working initially in Kenya. Along with other fellows,
Wise joined an emergency response team in the Philippines when
it was hit badly by Typhoon Haiyan in 2013. There he worked on
evaluating what worked well and what could be improved in future
emergency responses. Now Eric is back in Africa as a CRS field staff

---

1. "Meet Recent CRS Interns," Catholic Relief Services, *www.crs.org/about
/careers/internships/meet-recent-crs-interns*. CRS campus ambassadors' activities include
organizing awareness and advocacy programs focusing on global migration, conduct-
ing fundraising for global emergencies, and developing fair trade campaigns on cam-
puses. See "About Student Ambassadors," Catholic Relief Services, *www.university
.crs.org/students/about*.

member working on humanitarian aid and peace-building for internally displaced people in South Sudan.[2]

As a Georgetown undergraduate, Julia Leis worked with Burmese refugees in a school in northern Thailand. This led her to pursue a master's degree in international urban planning and development at Tufts University, where she had a number of internships and did field research in Haiti, Burkina Faso, and Kenya. Selected as a CRS international development fellow, Julia worked on a "Strengthen Urban Communities Capacity to Endure Severe Shocks" program, which builds community resilience with multiple strategies: creating savings and internal lending communities to help people save funds for emergencies; building waste management systems to control the spread of disease; and assisting community-shaped reconstruction of housing built to withstand repeated typhoons.[3]

Lorella Praeli was one of hundreds of thousands of DREAMers, people who were brought to the United States as children without proper authorization but for whom the United States is the only country they have ever known. "For years," Praeli says, "I learned to be quiet and to live in the shadows and to hide, and that my status was too dangerous to discuss in public. But I can no longer just sit and wait for something to happen without being involved in the process."[4] Praeli, along with hundreds of fellow DREAMers, began to "come out" in 2009 and 2010 in the run-up to a congressional vote on the DREAM act. "Where shame and isolation once dominated their ranks," Julianne Hing wrote in *The Nation*, "these young immigrants had come together and found power and pride in their shared identity and struggle."[5] Praeli did not quit when a Republican

---

2. "Speaking from Experience: Fellow Videos; Eric Wise, Kenya," Catholic Relief Services, *www.crs.org/about/careers/fellowships/fellow-experiences* (time: 0:01:55).

3. Ibid. See also Jessica Daniels, "First-Year Alumni: Julia Consolidates Her Interests in the Philippines," The Fletcher School, Tufts University, April 24, 2015, *http://sites.tufts.edu/fletcheradmissions/2015/04/24/first-year-alumni-julia-consolidates-her-interests-in-the-philippines/*; "Gallery: Living on Land That Is No Longer Land at All," Catholic Relief Services, *www.crs.org/stories/gallery-living-land-no-longer-land-all.*

4. Brent McDonald, "Pushing the Dream," *New York Times* (December 1, 2012), *www.nytimes.com/video/us/100000001929737/pushing-the-dream.html* (time: 0:07:41).

5. Julianne Hing, "The Young Activists Who Remade the Democratic Party's Immigration Politics," *The Nation*, January 21, 2016, *www.thenation.com/article/the-young-activists-who-remade-the-democratic-partys-immigration-politics.*

filibuster in the Senate killed the bill. She and many others confronted President Obama on his record number of deportations
and provided some of the grassroots pressure that led to his executive order, Deferred Action for Childhood Arrivals, in June 2012.
Through her activism, Praeli became politically savvy; she now works
as a Latino outreach coordinator on political campaigns.[6]

What these CRS interns and fellows share with Lorella Praeli is
that initial actions on issues of injustice and risk-taking led to a series
of life-changing deeper involvements with organizations that work on
behalf of marginalized people. They found or created for themselves a
"ladder of engagement," in which each rung climbed led to increasing
responsibility, reaching new heights of acquired competence.[7]

Examining What Leads to Action

It may be worth asking why some individuals choose to take action
but others do not. In a famous study, Samuel and Pearl Oliner
focused on the thousands of Europeans who rescued Jews from the
Nazi Holocaust. The Oliners immediately recognized that there
were a variety of motivations that impelled some Europeans to act,
even in such extreme circumstances, and differing ethical under-
standings that framed the actions of those engaged. Their study
offered three broad categories of rescuers. The first were those with a
strong empathic response to the suffering of others. For this group, a
sense of solidarity was a primary motivator, as these individuals frequently had previous friendships with Jews. A second group drew
its values from membership in a community, most often a religious
community. These individuals had a clear sense that God willed their
actions in spite of Nazi propaganda that demonized Jews. A third
group had a strongly internalized ethical framework. Individuals in
this group deeply believed that humans are created equal and are to
be treated as such. Many people who fell into one or another of these
categories, however, failed to act. For example, many nonrescuers had

---

6. Ibid.

7. CRS programs, in fact, offer this type of ladder of engagement—leading from
work as a campus ambassador to internships both at home and abroad and finally
to international development fellowships. See "Careers at CRS," Catholic Relief Services, *www.crs.org/about/careers*.

a strong empathic reaction to others' suffering, but recoiled from the pain that others' suffering caused them to feel and drew back into their own shell. Those who acted, however, exhibited a sense of most or all of the following character traits:

- **Personal Efficacy:** the belief that one's actions could create meaningful change, even if helping only one person survive.
- **Personal Responsibility:** the belief that one not only could effect change but that one must do so, however small an act might be. Both the sense of personal efficacy and personal responsibility are implied in the theological-ethical concept of stewardship.
- **Personal Integrity:** the belief that not to act means failing to be the person one wants to be. Such a person might say, "I want to act so as to be able to live with myself."
- **Inclusivity:** the belief that one is more similar to marginalized or demonized groups than different—that all share a common humanity.[8]

To be sure, rescuers developed these core character traits through many small steps. The Oliners say, "The moral life is not something to be switched on at a particular crisis, but it is something that goes on continually in the small piecemeal habits of living."[9] Consider the risk that Lorella Praeli was taking in coming out publicly about her immigration status. Such actions, the Oliners say, do not come out of the blue.

Taking Stock, Taking Initiative

Part 1 of this book, the "see" section, analyzed the current forces driving migration; looked at the predicament of refugees and asylum seekers, internally displaced people, and climate change refugees; and examined the pros and cons of immigration to America. This step was carried out at length because judging without first looking more

---

8. Samuel Oliner and Pearl Oliner, *The Altruistic Personality* (New York: Free Press, 1988). See especially chapters 7 and 8.

9. Ibid., 222.

deeply inevitably means projecting our own preconceptions and prejudices, often unconsciously, onto the issues that global migration raises. In a climate of fear, this leads to demonizing whole groups of people. Most importantly, not "seeing" means remaining blind to the multiple ways in which we are complicit in creating the conditions that force others to leave their homes. "Seeing" involves realizing how connected human beings are, which necessarily leads to reflection on one's own moral responsibility.

Part 2, the "judge" section, presented an ethical framework drawn from Catholic social teaching to guide in the development of a personal moral framework. Since ethical reflection that does not lead to action is an exercise in abstraction, the "judge" section was followed by the "act" section, part 3. Collective action, whether by humanitarian aid and development organizations like CRS, international agencies like the United Nations High Commissioner for Refugees, or advocacy groups seeking immigration reform, is critical in empowering refugees and migrants and pressuring powerful institutions like the U.S. Congress. But collective action is formed of the millions of actions by ordinary human beings.

CRS repeatedly stresses that its actions need to be *with* not *for* refugees and migrants; action needs to empower those who are migrating. The stories that opened this chapter have shown that it is possible to develop one's skills and moral character by acting with and for refugees and migrants. There can be a process of mutual empowerment. Each person has unique opportunities, strengths, and communities of influence and activity where the millions of actions can take place. Consider for a moment: What might your story look like? If you come from a background of service work or a community where these opportunities abound, what are you able to do? If you do not belong to such communities, how might you open yourself up to engaging on these issues? As mentioned in chapter 5, Liz Collier learned about these issues when she decided to do one year of service work with the Jesuit Volunteer Corps. There are many domestic and international volunteer opportunities, both faith-based and nonsectarian, where myriad justice issues are addressed.

This raises a number of questions for consideration. What needs to be done that you are capable of doing? What is needed that draws upon and strengthens your own assets? What strategies appeal to you as most effective, as well as suited to your strengths? Are these strategies sustainable? Understanding one's own capabilities also indicates what is a realistic level of commitment. Think about how Lorella Praeli and the CRS interns and fellows discussed at the beginning of this chapter found or constructed a ladder of engagement. Who are your allies? Who will support your efforts? Are there campus groups that you can join? With what organizations elsewhere could you network? What will you leave behind when you graduate? Are there others whom you can encourage to assume leadership of your campus endeavors? Undoubtedly, you can add to this list of questions and come to a decision about how to act that is suited to your interests and abilities.

In the Steps of Abraham

This book began with the story of Abram called by God to leave the city of Ur and migrate to a new land (Gen. 12). But the same chapter takes Abraham's story to the next stage when he is forced, by famine, to take refuge in Egypt for a time. Today, Daniel Pasquini-Salazar, a CRS international development fellow, works with sheep and goat herders in the West Bank where Abraham grazed his sheep.

Overgrazed rangeland, encroaching urbanization, and endemic conflict have led these Bedouin herders, like Abraham, to become

As a CRS international development fellow, Daniel Pasquini-Salazar works with local community organizations and Bedouin herders, like Hussein, to develop water conservation strategies and to restore overgrazed pastures.

"food-insecure" and at risk of becoming internally displaced persons. Daniel and CRS's local partner organization put CRS's guiding principles to work with these, "the most vulnerable population in the West Bank." They work with herders to develop soil and water conservation strategies, thereby building the community's capacity. Balancing people's need for food with preservation of the environment, and working through local partners while respecting people's right to self-determination, Daniel has learned valuable lessons about how to act well in challenging circumstances.[10] Learning to act well in challenging circumstances is a task for all people.

Reflect and Discuss

1. What questions do you have now that you have read this text? Which aspect of global migration particularly concerns you? What more do you need to know? Research this topic using supplementary readings. Write a brief essay distilling your expanded understanding of the issue based on your additional reading.

2. Work alone to review and address some of the questions, summarized in this chapter, that can encourage people to take action. Then, working in a small group, share your thoughts and ideas about action in response to issues of global migration. Ask, what actions have I done to date that have enhanced my sense of personal efficacy? What do I feel called upon to do at this moment? How might I find a ladder of engagement with issues that matter to me?

3. Research some organizations on campus that deal with the predicament of refugees, asylum seekers, and internally displaced persons. Research some organizations that deal with issues related to immigration to the United States. Do an analysis of similar organizations in your local community. Given their different missions and strategies, which of these do you feel best suits your own strengths and level of commitment?

---

10. "Fellow Experiences," Catholic Relief Services, *www.crs.org/about/careers /fellowships/fellow-experiences*; "Current Fellow—Daniel Pasquini-Salazar's Work in the Jerusalem, West Bank and Gaza Region," *www.facebook.com/notes/812820168785855*.

Epilogue

Thinking and Acting Ethically in Difficult Times

As this book goes to press, the situation for both refugees and immigrants to the United States has become more dangerous. A new administration in Washington, D.C., has ordered a temporary ban on refugees and immigrants from six Muslim-majority nations and an indefinite ban on those from Syria. Even doctors, college teachers, science researchers, and those seeking emergency medical care are affected. The country is deeply divided on this issue, which is now before the courts. According to the Cardinal Archbishop of Chicago, Blasé Cupich, we have entered "a dark moment in U.S. history."[1] How should individuals and communities proceed as moral agents in such confusing times?

Before reacting, stop. In such ethically challenging circumstances, many people are moved by anger or fear to react hastily. Take time to pause and reflect using the see-judge-act method for ethical reflection.

Step 1: See. Inform yourself by viewing multiple perspectives on the ethical issues regarding migration. Good sources to check include the websites of Catholic Relief Services, Justice for Immigrants, and the Migration Policy Institute. The ban on refugees and immigrants from some Muslim-majority nations is only one of many ethically troubling issues outlined in this book. It is best to place each issue within a comprehensive context.

Seeing involves learning from history. A historical perspective can shed new light on ethical issues. For example, Benjamin Franklin's fears

---

1. "Statement of Cardinal Blasé J. Cupich, Archbishop of Chicago, on the Executive Order on Refugees and Migrants," Archdiocese of Chicago, January 29, 2017, *www.archchicago.org/statements/-/asset_publisher/a2jOvEeHcvDT/content/statement -statement-of-cardinal-blase-j-cupich-archbishop-of-chicago-on-the-executive-order -on-refugees-and-migrants?inher.*

in 1773 of being swamped by a horde of German immigrants, which were discussed in chapter 3, seem groundless to Americans today but did not seem so at the time; "nativist" fears have recurred repeatedly throughout U.S. history. It helps to use history to examine our fears.

The United States has often been a haven for refugees—but not always. In May 1939, the MS St. Louis sailed from Hamburg, Germany, with 935 mostly German Jews on board escaping the Nazi's iron grip. Cuba refused permission for the passengers to disembark. Then so did Miami. Cables requesting emergency visas sent to President Roosevelt went unanswered. The St. Louis returned to Europe, where the majority of the passengers landed in Belgium only months before the Nazi invasion. As a consequence, 254 of the passengers were murdered in Hitler's concentration camps.[2] Refugees today clearly share one trait with those German Jews: desperation. The St. Louis is a stain on U.S. history. The people we are turning away from our borders right now may well suffer a similar fate.

Step 2: Judge. A functioning moral GPS is helpful in difficult times. Students in courses that grapple with identifying just responses to unjust situations in light of the principles of Catholic social teaching have the opportunity to develop their personal moral GPS. What core commitments must be honored to be a moral agent of integrity? Drawing upon an ethical framework to judge the moral implications of current issues helps us to avoid knee-jerk reactions.

Step 3: Act. Action without ethical reflection is blind, but ethical reflection without action is pointless. In dealing with global migration, there are all kinds of actions that may be taken. Contacting the White House and one's congressional representatives, volunteering at a local nongovernmental organization that sponsors refugees, joining the Catholic Relief Services' "I am Migration" campaign, and taking part in nonviolent direct actions in opposition to unjust government policies are just a few options.

"It is time," Cardinal Cupich said, "to put aside fear and join together to recover who we are and what we represent to a world badly in need of hope and solidarity."[3]

---

2. "Voyage of the St Louis," U.S. Holocaust Memorial Museum, *www.ushmm.org /wlc/en/article.php?ModuleId=10005267.*

3. "Statement of Cardinal Blase J. Cupich."

Index

Note: An italicized *i*, *n*, or *s* following a page number indicates an illustration, footnote or sidebar, respectively.